INTERNATIONAL SERIES OF MONOGRAPHS IN
ANALYTICAL CHEMISTRY
GENERAL EDITORS: R. BELCHER AND L. GORDON

Volume 23

GAS CHROMATOGRAPHY OF METAL CHELATES

GAS CHROMATOGRAPHY

OF

METAL CHELATES

by

ROSS W. MOSHIER

and

ROBERT E. SIEVERS

Aerospace Research Laboratories, ARC
Wright-Patterson Air Force Base, Ohio

PERGAMON PRESS

OXFORD · LONDON · EDINBURGH · NEW YORK

PARIS · FRANKFURT

Pergamon Press Ltd., Headington Hill Hall, Oxford
4 & 5 Fitzroy Square, London W.1

Pergamon Press (Scotland) Ltd., 2 & 3 Teviot Place, Edinburgh 1

Pergamon Press Inc., 44-01 21st Street, Long Island City, New York 11101

Pergamon Press S.A.R.L., 24 rue des Ecoles, Paris 5e

Pergamon Press GmbH, Kaiserstrasse 75, Frankfurt-am-Main

First edition 1965

Library of Congress Catalog Card No. 65-15519

Printed in Great Britain by
J. W. Arrowsmith Ltd., Winterstoke Road, Bristol 3.

2287/65

CONTENTS

PREFACE

FROM little more than a dream first voiced less than a decade ago the concept of separating metal complexes by gas chromatography has developed at a remarkable pace. The technique now exhibits promise surpassing even the most optimistic early expectations. Sensitivity, selectivity, and speed are its hallmarks. A firm foundation has been laid and it is clear that the technique merits further thorough study to better establish its place in metal analysis and studies of metal coordination compounds. In this monograph we have attempted to describe the present state of knowledge and to delineate what we believe will be fruitful areas for future research.

The work will be of interest to two groups: 1. Analytical and inorganic chemists concerned with metal analysis and the study of metal coordination compounds; 2. Researchers in gas chromatography. It would be difficult to find two groups with less common backgrounds. Few of the first group have ever had occasion to use gas chromatography and those in the second group have not often concerned themselves with metal coordination chemistry. We felt that to be useful the book should be intelligible to both groups. Therefore we have tried to steer a middle course, avoiding as much as possible the esoteric language of either. No prior knowledge of gas chromatography is assumed, but some readers will find it profitable to study one of the several excellent volumes on theory and general practice in conjunction with this monograph. The subject is treated from the specialist's viewpoint and an effort was made to avoid duplicating unnecessarily the material already available in the general treatises.

In preparing the manuscript the first author assumed responsibility for Chapters 1, 4, the Appendix, and the last half of Chapter 3, while the remainder was prepared by the second author. We welcome constructive criticism in the hope that future writings will be benefitted thereby. We appreciate the numerous letters that have served to keep us abreast of progress in other laboratories.

Not only has this interchange often stimulated thinking along new lines, but also it has greatly reduced wasteful duplication of efforts.

There are many to whom we owe our gratitude. We wish to thank Professor Louis Gordon, who suggested that we write this monograph and has been a source of continuing encouragement during its preparation. We also thank our colleagues past and present who read portions of the manuscript and made numerous valuable suggestions for its improvement: Dr. S. C. Chattoraj, Dr. K. J. Eisentraut, Dr. R. G. Linck, J. E. Schwarberg, Dr. Brandes H. Smith, and Peggy F. Wifall. Our thanks go also to those who have given us access to data prior to its publication, in particular Professor R. S. Juvet, Jr., W. D. Ross, G. Wheeler, Dr. W. G. Scribner, Dr. N. J. Rose, Dr. J. Tadmor, Professor H. Gesser and Dr. D. K. Albert. Our deepest gratitude is due to our wives, Mary Moshier and Nancy Sievers, for their unfailing encouragement and for their patience during the many hours spent away from our families.

Dayton, Ohio   R. W. MOSHIER
October 1964   R. E. SIEVERS

CHAPTER 1

INTRODUCTION

GAS chromatography is basically a process for separating and
analyzing mixtures of volatile compounds. In this method the
components of a mixture are subjected to repeated partition between a gaseous, moving phase and a liquid or solid stationary
phase. The separation is based on differences in vapor pressure
and solubility. The component which is less soluble in the stationary
phase and more volatile at the operating temperature moves
through the column more rapidly than the component which is
more soluble in the stationary phase and less volatile. This meets
the requirements for many systems in which the components have
sufficient volatility and thermal stability. It has been very successful for organic compounds because, generally, such compounds
have these properties. However, there is great interest in using
gas chromatography in separating nonvolatile organic and inorganic materials. In order to use gas chromatography for non-
volatile compounds, the biochemist has converted them to volatile
compounds. For example, for analysis of the nonvolatile, higher
fatty acids, he converts them into their methyl esters. These
derivatives generally possess sufficient volatility to permit them
to be subjected to gas chromatography, and they differ sufficiently
in properties to permit separation by gas chromotography.

Although inorganic compounds are generally not so volatile as
are the organic compounds, gas chromatography has been employed with a number of inorganic compounds that do possess
the required properties. As will be seen from the following résumé,
conversion to more suitable derivatives is not needed when the
volatile compounds are of direct interest.

Although some metals are volatile enough for gas chromatography, little interest has been shown in application of the method
to the analysis or separation of mixtures of such metals. This is

probably owing to the high column temperatures that would be required, and the lack of suitable liquid stationary phases stable at elevated temperatures. However, it has been reported[1] that cadmium and zinc can be partially separated by means of gas chromatography at a column temperature of 620°.

A number of metal hydrides are sufficiently volatile to permit direct use. Gas chromatography has been employed to study the reaction mechanism involved in the formation of diborane[2–4], its pyrolysis products[5] and its oxidation products[6]. Mixtures of the germanium hydrides have been analyzed by gas chromatography using silicone fluid as the stationary phase[7–9]. Mixtures of silicon hydride and germanium hydride have been similarly studied[10].

The chlorides of tin, antimony, titanium, niobium and tantalum possess sufficient volatility for gas chromatography. The tetrachlorides of tin and titanium have been separated with n-hexadecane as the stationary phase[11]. A mixture of the chlorides of tin, titanium, niobium and tantalum has been resolved using squalane or n-octadecane as the stationary phase[12]. Tin tetrachloride and antimony trichloride have been separated using as the stationary phase the fused eutectic mixture, bismuth chloride–lead chloride[13]. The eutectic, cadmium chloride–potassium chloride, has been used for the same purpose; however, only partial resolution of tin and titanium tetrachlorides was obtained when the stationary phase was a fused mixture of aluminum chloride and sodium chloride[14]. Gas chromatography has been employed for the phosphorus chlorides[15–17] and for the polymeric phosphonitrile halides[18–20]. Application of gas chromatography to analysis of uranium hexafluoride and its associated corrosive gases in atomic energy processes has been reported[20–24].

Organic derivatives, other than chelates, which have been or are currently being investigated, include compounds of boron, silicon, tin, lead, phosphorus, arsenic, etc., having a carbon to metal linkage. Gas chromatographic studies have involved the methyldiboranes[25], the alkylated penta- and decaboranes[26–28], the boron trialkylenes[29], the reaction products of boranes with dienes[30], and the reaction products of boranes with various organoaluminum compounds[31]. In the field of silicon compounds, gas chromatography has been employed with the chloromethyl-silanes[32], the chloroethylsilanes[33], the chlorophenylsilanes[34], and the pyrolysis products of the tetramethylsilanes[35–36]. The products, bromotriethylsilane and bromotriethylgermane, of a Wurtz coupling reaction have been successfully determined[37], as well as tetramethylgermane[38] and the methylated germanosiloxanes[39].

Research with organotin compounds includes purification of perfluorovinyl tin compounds and their cleavage products by gas chromatography[40], separation of homologous di- and tetra-alkyltin compounds[41], and purification of the reaction products of perfluoroalkyl iodides with the alkyltin compounds[42–43]. Studies with the alkylleads include resolution of five alkyllead compounds used in gasoline[44–46] and purification of the reaction products of alkyllead compounds and perfluoroalkyl iodides[42–43]. The tetramethyl compounds of silicon, germanium, tin and lead showed a linear relationship of molecular weights and boiling points with respect to gas chromatographic retention times[47]. Gas chromatography has been successful for many triorganophosphines and phosphine oxides[48–49], the alkyl phosphites[50–51], and organo-arsines[52–54].

In general, the compounds mentioned above do not meet the requirements for application of gas chromatography to metal analysis because they are difficult to prepare in quantitative yields, and many of them are susceptible to hydrolysis. To apply gas chromatography to metal separation, metal purification and metal analysis, a large number of metals must readily react with a single reagent to give quantitative yields of the metal compounds. This class of compounds must possess several properties which meet the requirements for separation and analysis by gas chromatography. In Chapter 2 the properties of metal compounds which meet these requirements are discussed. Of these properties sufficient volatility and thermal stability are paramount.

Inspection of numerous classes of derivatives to which inorganic materials may be converted reveals only a few possibilities for successful gas chromatographic application. Of these may be mentioned the metal carbonyls, the metal alkoxides, the metal alkyls, and a few types of metal chelates. Of these classes of compounds, the metal chelates are of particular interest because they can be prepared to include almost any metallic element. Furthermore, the chelates can be formed in quantitative yields much more readily than other compounds and they are less susceptible to hydrolysis. The metal chelating agents contain as donor atoms such elements as oxygen, sulfur, selenium, phosphorus and nitrogen. Of the chelating agents, the β-diketones which contain oxygen donors form metal compounds with the volatility, solubility, and thermal stability requirements for successful gas chromatographic elution.

In considering the various oxidation states of metal ions it has been learned that the chelates of the di-, tri- and tetravalent metals with the β-diketones are the most suitable for gas chromatography. Of the β-diketones, acetylacetone, trifluoroacetylacetone, and hexafluoroacetylacetone form chelates having the desired volatility. Some do not possess the required thermal stability. In general the more highly fluorinated the diketone, the greater is the vapor pressure of its metal chelate. With fluorinated chelates the high volatility permits the gas chromatography of more metals than would otherwise be possible because high temperatures, which often lead to thermal degradation, are not required. The acetylacetonates of about sixty metals, and a lesser number of the trifluoro- and hexafluoroacetylacetonates have been prepared and characterized (see the Appendix, page 138).

It is the purpose of this book to present what has been learned concerning the use of volatile metal chelates in separation and analysis of metals by gas chromatography.

Since its inception in the late nineteen-fifties the application of gas chromatography to the metal chelates of the β-diketones has developed rapidly. The first studies were made by Gesser and co-workers[55-58] who accomplished the successful gas chromatographic elution of the acetylacetonates of beryllium, aluminum and chromium; and by Brandt and co-workers[59-63] who studied several metal β-diketonates. A detailed study of the gas chromatography of chromium(III) acetylacetonate was made to determine the accuracy of a quantitative determination[62-63]. The degree of analytical attainment was tested on a Bureau of Standards alloy. The results differed from the certified value by 3.3 per cent relative.

The gas chromotography of metal chelates has been expanded[64-77] to encompass elutions of not only additional metal acetylacetonates but also of many metal trifluoroacetylacetonates and metal hexafluoroacetylacetonates. They can be chromotagraphed at temperatures far below their boiling points. Conditions have been determined for the resolution of the peaks for many mixtures. Geometric and optical isomers have been resolved[69,71].

As with other gas chromatography procedures, consideration must be given to such factors as selection of the stationary phase, the solid support and the detector. A good stationary phase gives optimum resolution of peaks with minimum tailing. Choice of solid support for the stationary phase is also determined by the extent of tailing. In part, peak tailing is due to differing activities of adsorption sites in the column. Improvement in elution behaviour by reduction of tailing may be accomplished by inactivation of active sites on the solid support. Choice of the detector will depend upon the nature of the compound under study. For example, halogen in a molecule lowers the response of one detector whereas it enhances the response of another type detector. Also, for the same compound, some detectors are more sensitive than others; one may determine picogram quantities of a component using one detector, whereas another detector will be useful only for determining milligram or microgram quantities of the same component. Detector choice is an important consideration in the gas chromatography of metal chelates, as is shown in Chapter 3 which deals with the subject.

By the application of gas chromatography to the metal chelates of the β-diketones, many metal separations are readily accomplished. Separations which are lengthy and difficult are found impractical by other means may be relatively simple by gas chromatography. The separated metal chelates are readily isolated by a simple trapping arrangement which serves to collect each metal chelate as it emerges in the effluent stream from the instrument.

The requirements for the quantitative gas chromatography of metal chelates are discussed in Chapter 4. Applied to metal chelates the technique is one of the most rapid analytical methods because of the simplicity in the preparation of the compounds, the rapidity with which chromatograms are obtained, and the ease of measuring the quantities present. It readily eliminates troublesome separation procedures necessary in many accepted analytical methods. As more metal chelates are prepared and studied, the extent of usefulness of the method to metal analysis will be better established.

REFERENCES

1. F. E. DE BOER, *Nature*, **185**, 915 (1960).
2. H. W. MYERS and R. F. PUTNAM, *Anal. Chem.*, **34**, 664 (1962).
3. G. SCHOMBURG, 4th International Gas Chromatography Symposium, Hamburg, June 13–16, 1962.
4. A. B. LITTLEWOOD, Symposium on Gas Chromatography, Society for Analytical Chemistry, Edinburgh, Scotland (May 1955).
5. K. BORER, A. B. LITTLEWOOD and C. S. G. PHILLIPS, *J. Inorg. Nuclear Chem.*, **15**, 316 (1960).
6. E. GOBBETT and J. W. LINNETT, *J. Chem. Soc.*, 2893 (1962).
7. J. E. DRAKE and W. L. JOLLY, *Proc. Chem. Soc.*, 379 (1961).
8. J. E. DRAKE and W. L. JOLLY, 141st National Meeting, American Chemical Society, Washington, D.C., March 1962.
9. J. E. DRAKE and W. L. JOLLY, *J. Chem. Soc.*, 2807 (1962).
10. C. S. G. PHILLIPS and P. L. TIMMS, *Anal. Chem.*, **35**, 505 (1963).
11. H. FREISER, *Anal. Chem.*, **31**, 1440 (1959).
12. R. A. KELLER, *J. Chromatog.*, **5**, 225 (1961).
13. R. S. JUVET and F. M. WACHI, *Anal. Chem.*, **32**, 290 (1960).
14. F. M. WACHI, Thesis, Univ. of Illinois, 1959.
15. S. H. SHIPOTOFSKY and H. C. MOSER, *Anal. Chem.*, **33**, 521 (1961).
16. F. G. STANFORD, *J. Chromatog.*, **4**, 419 (1960).
17. M. LE SECH, Journées Internationales d'Etude des Méthodes de Separation Immediate et de Chromatographie, June 13–15, 1961, Paris, France.
18. A. C. CHAPMAN, N. L. PADDOCK, D. H. PAINE, H. T. SEARLE and D. R. SMITH, *J. Chem. Soc.*, 3608 (1960).
19. F. G. R. GIMLETT, *Chem. and Ind.*, (London) 365 (1958).
20. G. IVESON, United Kingdom, Atomic Energy Comm. PG Report 82, 1–15 (1960); *Gas Chromatog. Proc. Symposium*, 3rd, Edinburgh, Scotland (1960), pp. 333–43.
21. J. V. ELLIS and C. W. FORREST, *J. Inorg. Nuclear Chem.*, **16**, 150 (1960).
22. J. F. ELLIS, C. W. FORREST and P. L. ALLEN, *Anal. Chim. Acta.*, **22**, 27 (1960).
23. T. R. PHILLIPS and D. R. OWENS, *3rd Symposium on Gas Chromatography*, Edinburgh, Scotland, June 8–10, 1960. Butterworths, 1960, pp. 146–153.
24. A. G. HAMLIN, G. IVESON and T. R. PHILLIPS, *Anal. Chem.*, **35**, 2037 (1963).
25. G. R. SEELY, J. P. OLIVER and D. M. RITTER, *Anal. Chem.*, **31**, 1993 (1959).
26. N. J. BLAY, I. DUNSTAN and R. L. WILLIAMS, *J. Chem., Soc.*, 430, (1960); 5006 (1960).
27. N. J. BLAY, J. WILLIAMS and R. L. WILLIAMS, *J. Chem. Soc.*, 424, (1960).

28. L. J. Kuhns, R. S. Braman and J. E. Graham, *Anal. Chem.*, **34**, 1700 (1962).
29. G. Schomburg, R. Köster and D. Henneberg, *Z. Anal. Chem.*, **170**, 285 (1959).
30. G. Zweifel, K. Nagase and H. C. Brown, *J. Am. Chem. Soc.*, **84**, 183 (1962).
31. R. Köster and G. Bruno, *Ann.*, **629**, 89 (1960).
32. Chung-Chien Hsien, H-C Yang, F-C Su, Chen-Chen Hsien and C-H Liu, *Acta Chim. Sinica*, **25**, 420 (1959).
33. J. Joklik, *Coll. Czech. Chem. Commun.*, **26**, 2079 (1961).
34. J. Franc and M. Wurst, *Coll. Czech. Chem. Commun.*, **25**, 701 (1960).
35. G. Fritz and J. Grobe, *Z. anorg. allgem. Chem.*, **315**, 157 (1962).
36. G. Fritz, J. Grobe and D. Ksinsik, *Z. anorg. allgem. Chem.*, **302**, 175 (1959).
37. J. M. Shackelford, H. De Schmertzing, C. H. Heuther and H. Podall, *J. Org. Chem.*, **28**, 1700 (1963).
38. J. I. Peterson, L. M. Kindley and H. E. Podall, Pittsburgh Conference on Analytical Chemistry and Applied Spectroscopy, March 4–8, 1963.
39. H. Schmidbauer and M. Schmidt, *Chem. Ber.*, **94**, 1138, 2137 (1961).
40. H. D. Kaesz, S. L. Stafford and F. G. A. Stone, *J. Am. Chem. Soc.*, **82**, 6232 (1960).
41. J. Franc, M. Wurst and V. Moudry, *Coll. Czech. Chem. Commun.*, **26**, 1313 (1961).
42. H. D. Kaesz, J. R. Phillips and F. G. A. Stone, *J. Am. Chem. Soc.*, **82**, 6228 (1960).
43. J. R. Phillips and F. G. A. Stone, Pittsburgh Conference on Anal. Chem. and Applied Spectroscopy, March 4–8, 1963.
44. W. W. Parker, G. Z. Smith and R. L. Hudson, *Anal. Chem.*, **33**, 1170 (1961).
45. J. E. Lovelock and A. Zlatkis, *Anal. Chem.*, **33**, 1958 (1961).
46. R. E. Laramy, L. D. Lively and G. Perkins, Jr., Pittsburgh Conference on Anal. Chem. and Applied Spectroscopy, Mar. 5–9, 1962.
47. E. W. Abel, G. Nickless and F. H. Pollard, *Proc. Chem. Soc.*, 288 (1960).
48. B. J. Gudzinowicz and R. H. Campbell, *Anal. Chem.*, **33**, 1510 (1961).
49. S. A. Buckler, *J. Am. Chem. Soc.*, **84**, 3093 (1962).
50. A. Davis, A. Roaldi, J. G. Michalovic and H. M. Joseph, 14th Mid-Atlantic Spectroscopy Symposium, Chicago, May 20–23 (1963).
51. S. H. Shipotofsky, U.S. Atomic Energy Comm. TID-6437, 22 pp., 1960.
52. B. J. Gudzinowicz and H. F. Martin, *Anal. Chem.*, **34**, 648 (1960).
53. B. J. Gudzinowicz, R. H. Campbell, J. L. Driscoll and H. F. Martin, Pittsburgh Conference on Anal. Chem. and Applied Spectroscopy, Mar. 4–8, 1963.
54. B. J. Gudzinowicz and J. L. Driscoll, *J. Gas Chromatog.*, **1**, 25 (May 1963).
55. W. J. Biermann and H. Gesser, *Anal. Chem.*, **32**, 1525 (1960).
56. W. G. Baldwin, Masters Thesis, Univ. of Manitoba (1961).
57. R. D. Hill, Masters Thesis, Univ. of Manitoba (1962).
58. R. D. Hill and H. Gesser, *J. Gas Chromatog.*, **1**, 11 (Oct. 1963).
59. A. A. Duswalt, Jr., Doctoral Dissertation, Purdue Univ. (1958).

60. W. V. FLOUTZ, Masters Thesis, Purdue Univ. (1959).
61. R. G. MELCHER, Masters Thesis, Purdue Univ. (1961).
62. J. E. HEVERAN, Masters Thesis, Purdue Univ. (1962).
63. W. W. BRANDT and J. E. HEVERAN, 142nd National Meeting, American Chemical Society, Atlantic City, N.J., Sept. 9–14, 1962.
64. R. E. SIEVERS, R. W. MOSHIER and B. W. PONDER, 141st National Meeting, American Chemical Society, Washington, D.C., March 1962.
65. R. E. SIEVERS, B. W. PONDER, M. L. MORRIS and R. W. MOSHIER, Inorg. Chem., 2, 693 (1963).
66. W. D. ROSS, Anal. Chem., 35, 1596 (1963); W. D. ROSS and G. WHEELER, JR., Anal. Chem., 36, 266 (1964).
67. J. E. SCHWARBERG, Masters Thesis, University of Dayton (1964).
68. J. E. SCHWARBERG, R. W. MOSHIER and J. H. WALSH, Talanta, 11, 1213 (1964).
69. R. W. MOSHIER, J. E. SCHWARBERG, M. L. MORRIS, and R. E. SIEVERS, Pittsburgh Conference on Analytical Chemistry and Applied Spectroscopy, Pittsburgh, Pa., Mar. 4–8, 1963.
70. R. E. SIEVERS, 16th Annual Summer Symposium on Analytical Chemistry Tucson, Arizona, June 19, 1963.
71. R. E. SIEVERS, R. W. MOSHIER and M. L. MORRIS, Inorg. Chem., 1, 966 (1962).
72. R. S. JUVET and R. P. DURBIN, J. Gas Chromatography, 1, 14 (Dec. 1963).
73. D. K. ALBERT, Anal. Chem., 36, 2034 (1964).
74. T. FUJINAGA, T. KUWAMOTO and Y. ONO, Bunseki Kagaku, 12, (12), 1199 (1963); C.A., 60, 6209 (1964).
75. K. YAMAKAWA, K. TANIKAWA and K. ARAKAWA, Chem. Pharm. Bull. (Tokyo), 11, (11), 1405 (1963); C.A., 60, 7464 (1964).
76. R. G. LINCK and R. E. SIEVERS, 148th National Meeting, American Chemical Society, Chicago, Ill., Sept. 1964.
77. W. D. ROSS, R. E. SIEVERS and G. WHEELER, JR., Anal. Chem., 37, 598 (1965).

CHAPTER 2

GENERAL CONSIDERATIONS

DURING the past few years workers in several laboratories have started the study of the application of gas chromatography to metal analysis. This concept requires that a mixture of metals or metal compounds be converted to volatile compounds which can then be subjected to gas chromatographic separation and measurement. The greatest obstacle has been in finding suitable volatile compounds for this purpose. If this difficulty could be surmounted, it was reasoned that the technique might well replace many of the existing methods for analyzing mixtures of metals. Gas chromatography, one of the most powerful tools available to the chemist, is capable of separating complex mixtures rapidly and of detecting the components at remarkably low levels. The extraordinary sensitivity of the technique is one of its most attractive features. By use of one of the advanced ionization detectors, quantities in the nanogram to picogram range are readily detectable.

Furthermore, there is a degree of versatility in gas chromatography not evident in other techniques. By the simple expedient of changing one of the parameters, for example, the column temperature or the liquid stationary phase, the nature of the data can be improved markedly. Resolution can be enhanced and the analysis time shortened by simple parameter changes. In many other analytical measurements, the nature of data presentation is fixed. In ultraviolet or infrared spectroscopy, for example, a given sample will yield a particular fixed plot of absorbance vs. wavelength. If the data presented are unsuitable because of interferences or insufficient sensitivity, etc., the only alternative is to alter the sample by removing the interferences, changing the ligand, or some other operation. In gas chromatography, on the other hand, the data presentation as manifested by the chromatograms can be changed markedly by simple variations in conditions without performing any operations on the sample itself. Should these fail, all the standard sample treatment options are still open to the analyst.

The wide variety of detectors available makes it possible to take advantage of specificity in response characteristic of selected detection techniques. Two examples should illustrate the importance of this aspect. The electron capture detector is remarkably sensitive to halogenated compounds, yet insensitive to hydrocarbons. This permitted Ross and Wheeler[1,2] to detect ultratrace amounts of chromium hexafluoroacetylacetonate in toluene solution with no interference by the large amounts of solvent present. Similarly, Juvet and Durbin[3] used a flame spectrophotometric detector which responds selectively depending on the wavelength at which the detector is operated. This is particularly valuable if it happens that two or more chelates cannot be completely separated. The detector is operated at a given wavelength to measure one component of the mixture and at another wavelength in a subsequent chromatographic run to measure the other component (see p. 69).

The versatility of gas chromatography is further enhanced by the ease with which it may be combined with other techniques to solve especially difficult problems of separation or measurement. Solvent extraction affords an excellent illustration, for if two components cannot be readily separated by gas chromatography, often one of these may be removed during the preliminary sample preparation step by varying any one of several conditions (pH, addition of masking agents, etc.) associated with the extraction. Brandt and Heveran[4] have demonstrated this versatility in their work on the determination of trace quantities of chromium(III) acetylacetonate. Under the chromatographic conditions which they employed, iron(III) and other metals interfered with the determination. To obviate the difficulty, they extracted the chelates with carbon disulfide and then back-extracted the interfering metals with 10 per cent hydrochloric acid.

COMPOUND REQUIREMENTS

In the subsequent discussion it will be seen that gas chromatography, with the variety of elegant detectors available combined with the simple yet potent separation process, is a remarkably valuable tool. However, there are a number of requirements that must be met if the technique is to be successfully applied to metal analysis.

Volatility*

The most important and restricting requirement is that the compounds be volatile enough to be chromatographed in the gas phase. Fortunately, this consideration is not as demanding as it may at first seem. It is not necessary to operate the column above the boiling point of the metal compound for elution to occur, because a compound need only possess vapor pressure on the order of a few millimeters at the temperature at which the column is operated to be eluted reasonably rapidly. Only a few types of metal compounds meet this requirement. Immediately eliminated are most types of charged or highly polar species in which intermolecular forces are high. Though possibly at sufficiently high temperatures even these could be chromatographed, experimental difficulties will probably render this impractical for the immediately forseeable future. What contributes to volatility is hard to define, and it is much easier to specify the factors that reduce vapor pressure than to attempt to designate those that increase it. The existence of large dipoles, adduct formation, polymerization, hydrogen bonding, and other factors will act to reduce volatility. The types of metal compounds that are volatile at reasonably low temperatures are limited in number. They include metal halides, metal alkoxides, metal carbonyls, metal alkyls, metal hydrides, π-bonded metal complexes such as the metal cyclopentadienyls and various metal chelates, e.g. β-diketonates and porphyrins. For reasons that will become apparent as the other factors are considered, the most promising candidates for use in metal analysis

---

* Confusion often arises from the use of the term "volatility". Because each compound gives a unique plot of vapor pressure as a function of temperature, one compound may have a higher vapor pressure than another compound at one temperature but a lower vapor pressure at another. For gas chromatography, prime concern is placed on the vapor pressure range (estimated to be on the order of 1–10 mm) which permits moderately rapid elution from the types of columns used in the studies described. In the subsequent discussion a compound will be described as being more volatile than another if it possesses a higher vapor pressure at the temperature of the column.

are the metal chelates of β-diketones (especially the fluorinated derivatives), and in some instances the metal halides.

Stability

The importance of the stability of a compound is strongly dependent on its volatility. More volatile compounds can be eluted at lower column temperatures with the result that thermal stability requirements are not as demanding. For quantitative work the compounds should be sufficiently thermally stable that they can be eluted without degradation. However, in certain circumstances it may be possible to obtain quantitative data even though decomposition is apparent. This can be obtained when the extent of decomposition is slight, and occurs to the same extent under a given set of conditions regardless of the nature of the sample and the identity of the other components present in a mixture. Obviously this practice has its risks, so if decomposition does occur, it will be necessary to establish its reproducibility for every mixture anticipated before data can be interpreted with confidence. The best indication of thermal degradation is obtained by examining the injection port after a sample has been injected. The presence of a residue suggests one of two things. Either decomposition is occurring or the injection port temperature is not high enough to cause rapid sample vaporization. By varying the injection port temperature one can establish which is the case. Other danger signals indicating decomposition are the appearance of spurious chromatographic peaks, irregular baselines and discoloration of the column packing material.

A further important test of decomposition is made by collecting and identifying the eluted samples. It is imperative that the identity of the eluate be established if the data are to be interpreted unambiguously. Many of the uncertainties and apparent contradictions existing in the literature would not have appeared if such tests had been made. In every new system eluate fractions should be collected and identified by an independent test such as by measuring the melting point or ultraviolet spectrum to insure that a given peak is caused, in fact, by the compound injected rather than a decomposition product. Methods for identifying the eluate fractions are discussed further in Chapter 3.

In addition to being thermally stable, the compounds must be solvolytically stable when dissolved in the liquid stationary phase in the column. If the liquid phase can compete effectively as a coordinating agent, solvolysis will occur. The compounds should also be nonreactive with the solid stationary support and with the materials of construction of the chromatographic flow system. From a practical standpoint, it is desirable that the compounds be stable in the ambient atmosphere, so as to avoid special handling procedures.

Unlike the thermal stability requirement, there are ways of circumventing some of the other stability requirements. Careful selection of non-reactive liquid partitioning phases, solid supports and materials for construction of columns will permit greater flexibility in operation. It is burdensome to work with compounds such as the metal halides that undergo hydrolysis in the atmosphere, but the problems are not insurmountable.

Finally, there is one other consideration which is rarely of concern but should be mentioned nevertheless. The components of the sample should not undergo mutual reaction. For example, redox reactions may occur if oxidizing and reducing species are present in a mixture. Occasionally dimerization or polymerization may present a problem, particularly when hydroxo, oxo, chloro, etc., bridge formation can occur. Therefore, wherever possible, it is advantageous to work with compounds that are coordinatively saturated and do not contain moieties that readily form bridges.

Ease of Formation

For quantitative work the types of compounds which can be used are limited to those that can be readily formed in quantitative or nearly quantitative and easily reproducible yield. It is this factor that disqualifies several of the classes of volatile compounds listed earlier. The metal carbonyls, hydrides and alkyls are usually formed only with difficulty and rarely in quantitative yield. Their syntheses cannot be carried out in water owing to the solvolytic instability of the products. On the other hand, certain chelating agents form complexes of high solvolytic stability by simple reactions that readily occur. The reactions can be carried out in aqueous or non-aqueous media and are pH dependent, a feature affording a measure of selectivity in handling difficultly separable mixtures. In the case of β-diketone chelates there are still other attractive features. Many of the metal ions form complexes under similar conditions, simplifying the sample preparation procedure. Metal β-diketonates also lend themselves well to solvent extraction with its attendant advantages in selectivity.

At first glance it might seem that the anhydrous metal halides would be difficult to form by any convenient route. It will not be possible to use aqueous samples directly, but there are some approaches that may be useful. Keulemans[5] has reported that many compounds can be converted to metal chlorides by grinding them with carbon and chlorinating at a temperature of about 1000°C. It has been suggested[6] that an easier method involves the direct reaction of metal oxides with carbon tetrachloride. At temperatures of the order of 300–400°C carbon tetrachloride is an excellent chlorinating agent[7], as in the following reaction:

$$TiO_2 + 2CCl_4 \rightarrow TiCl_4 + 2COCl_2$$

The reaction can be effected conveniently in a sealed borosilicate glass tube, and is quantitative for a surprisingly large number of metals. It has recently been reported[8] that metal sulfides can also be converted to the chlorides by reaction with carbon tetrachloride at elevated temperatures, offering still another possible route.

Special Properties

In some instances it is desirable to incorporate special properties into the compounds undergoing chromatographic analysis. Ross[1] has demonstrated that the electron capture detector is capable of detecting much smaller amounts of fluorine-containing chelates than of the analogous unfluorinated compounds. The electronegative fluorine atoms in the chelates function as excellent electron-capturing species and improve the sensitivity by a factor greater than 100, permitting the detection of quantities of chromium on the order of 10^{-12} g. For the same reason the electron capture detector should exhibit extraordinary sensitivity in detecting metal halides.

Another property that might be incorporated into β-diketone complexes is radioactivity. By forming a complex with a labeled ligand, one might expect to achieve highly sensitive detection and extend analyses to ultra-trace quantities using radioactive detectors. This technique has been used successfully on labeled organic compounds by Evans and Willard[9], who showed it was possible to detect amounts of the order of 10^{-13} to 10^{-15} g. In spite of the experimental inconveniences of handling labeled compounds, the sensitivity expected will doubtless stimulate work in this area. Tadmor[10,11] has described a clever technique for labeling compounds while they are in the chromatographic column, thereby eliminating the necessity for prior labeling. In these experiments metal chlorides were labeled as they were separated and determined. The stationary phase had previously been labelled with ^{36}Cl, so that as the metal chlorides passed through the column, chlorine exchange occurred to yield high specific-activity labeled compounds. The possible combination of gas chromatography with neutron activation analysis is another approach that merits study.

GAS CHROMATOGRAPHIC SEPARATIONS

Metal Acetylacetonates

In 1955 Lederer[12] first suggested the separation of metal acetylacetonates by gas chromatography. Though a number of metal acetylacetonates are known to be somewhat volatile, with a few exceptions the results obtained have not been encouraging. Duswalt[13] reported that chromatographic peaks were obtained when chromatography of solutions of beryllium, scandium and zinc acetylacetonates was attempted. The retention times for all three complexes were virtually identical. However, Floutz,[14] another student in the same laboratory, was unable to duplicate the experiments. He was successful in obtaining a chromatographic peak for the beryllium chelate, but not for the scandium or zinc complexes. He suggested that the peaks obtained in the earlier study for the scandium and zinc chelates were due to traces of beryllium in the scandium and zinc samples. But it is also possible that sample decomposition in one or both of the studies gave rise to the discrepancies. Fujinaga, Kuwamoto and Ono[15] have given a brief preliminary report on their recent study of scandium(III) acetylacetonate. They claim that flash vaporization chamber temperatures between 200 and 310°C can be used for this complex without apparent decomposition.* With the temperature of the column at 220°C chromatograms showing reasonably sharp peaks were obtained. The peak areas were linearly related to the amount of solid scandium(III) acetylacetonate introduced over the range from 0.7 to 5 mg.

The data obtained for the aluminum and chromium(III) acetylacetonates are quite extensive[1,4,14,16–23]. Both complexes can be eluted under widely varying conditions without any apparent decomposition. The chromatogram in Fig. 2.1 shows the separation of a mixture of these chelates[17]. The chelates were dissolved in carbon tetrachloride and the solution was injected into a column maintained at 170°C. The aluminum chelate was eluted prior to the chromium chelate as expected on the basis of its greater volatility.

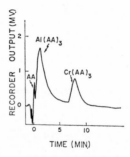

Fig. 2.1. Separation of aluminum and chromium(III) acetylacetonates [17]. *Sample*: 0.34 μl. of a CCl₄ soln. of the chelates. *Column temp.*: 170°C. *Column*: 4 ft × ¼ in., containing 1 per cent Apiezon L on glass microbeads. *Argon flow rate*: 43 ml min⁻¹.
(Courtesy of *Analytical Chemistry*)

In addition to the beryllium, aluminum, and chromium acetylacetonates, the complexes of copper(II), vanadium(IV) and iron(III) also have been chromatographed successfully[16–24]. Column temperatures between 150 and 200°C were required for the compounds to be eluted in reasonable time periods. For each of the

---

* The metal complex was introduced into the flash vaporization chamber in crystalline form rather than in solution as is customary.

chelates, and for the beryllium, aluminum, and chromium(III) chelates as well, samples were condensed from the eluate stream in a sample collecting device immersed in a solid carbon dioxide–acetone bath. The collected fractions were identified by comparing melting points or ultraviolet spectra with those of authentic samples of the chelates.

Unfortunately, however, many of the other metal acetylacetonates are not sufficiently volatile to be eluted without decomposing. At low column temperatures movement of the chelates through the column is imperceptible, and at higher temperatures thermal decomposition or solvolytic reaction occurs. Above 200°C thermal degradation becomes a problem for all but the most stable chelates. Attempts to chromatograph acetylacetonate complexes of zirconium(IV), hafnium(IV), cobalt(III), thorium(IV) and titanium(IV) at column temperatures between 150 and 230°C were unsuccessful[16]. At the lower temperatures only one peak, attributed to the solvent, is produced. At the higher temperatures the compounds sometimes decompose to give spurious peaks in the chromatograms. When a chelate decomposes rapidly to yield a volatile product, the decomposition product may appear as a well-defined peak in the chromatogram. In most instances volatile decomposition products are eluted much more rapidly than the chelates and are either obscured by the solvent or appear as a shoulder on the solvent peak, but occasionally they produce a distinct peak with a retention time similar to those obtained for the stable chelates. One illustration will emphasize the necessity for identifying the eluate. During an attempt to chromatograph cobalt(III) acetylacetonate a sharp, well-defined peak, distinct from the solvent peak, appeared in the chromatogram[16]. Collection and examination of the eluate revealed, however, that the peak in question was caused by a decomposition product rather than by the chelate. This illustrates how easy it might be to arrive at incorrect conclusions when sufficient evidence regarding the identity of the eluate is not obtained.

The recent work of Yamakawa, Tanikawa and Arakawa[25] should be discussed because it appears to stand in contradiction to previously published reports. The reader is cautioned against relying on the *Chemical Abstracts* version of the study because it is misleadingly incomplete. Examination of the original paper reveals that the contradictions are more apparent than real. Twenty metal acetylacetonates were studied in varying degrees. It was found that beryllium, aluminum, chromium(III) and vanadyl acetylacetonates easily gave sharp chromatographic peaks at column temperatures between 150 and 180°C, in complete agreement with earlier published reports. Although the conditions used were not identical with those in previous studies, they were similar enough to be comparable. The Japanese workers also obtained peaks for the cobalt(III), magnesium, manganese(II), barium, calcium, cadmium(II), molybdenyl(II), titanium(III), thorium, zinc and zirconium complexes, and reported retention volumes for all except cobalt(III). No mention was made of any efforts to verify that the complexes were eluted intact. Other observations tend to make one suspect that at least some if not most of the peaks obtained for the latter group of compounds were caused by decomposition products. The authors were careful to point out that, while the chromatograms of the beryllium, aluminum, chromium and vanadyl chelates showed sharp peaks and the appearance of the peaks was not influenced by varying the column temperatue and carrier gas flow rate, it was difficult to select conditions to obtain stable chromatograms for the magnesium, manganese(II) and cobalt(III) chelates. They also remarked that the peaks were broad for the barium, calcium, cadmium(II), molybdenyl(II), titanium(III), thorium, zinc and zirconium complexes. Provoking further concern about whether or not elution of the complexes actually occurred is the observation that several of the complexes have the same (within experimental error) retention times. This would suggest that the peaks may be caused by decomposition products common to several of the complexes. The work of Charles and co-workers[26,27] lends indirect support to this conclusion. They showed that many of the metal acetylacetonates undergo substantial thermal decomposition on heating in an inert atmosphere at 191°C for one hour. The zirconium, cobalt(II), zinc, cadmium and strontium complexes are among the least thermally stable, based on the amount of evolved gaseous decomposition products. The gaseous products, identified by their mass spectra, are primarily acetone and carbon dioxide. In some cases acetylacetone and methane were also principal decomposition products.

In summary, based on the evidence now available, the acetylacetonates do not appear to be sufficiently volatile and stable to be as broadly useful in metal analysis as one might wish. For certain elements, particularly beryllium, aluminum and chromium, the situation is brighter. Separations of mixtures of these three metal acetylacetonates have been accomplished with a variety of columns and conditions[14,16,18,21,22]. Quantitative studies on these chelates, both individually and as mixtures, have been made, and there is no question that they are sufficiently stable to yield reliable quantitative data[4,21,28] (see Chapter 4).

Obviously, much work of a definitive nature remains to be done before we will have an accurate picture of the acetylacetonates. The confusion surrounding the behavior of some of these compounds can be eliminated only by repeating the studies to obtain more conclusive evidence regarding the identity of the eluted compounds.

Fluorocarbon β-diketonate Chelates

It can readily be seen from the foregoing section that it was necessary to find more volatile classes of metal compounds. The search conducted at the Aerospace Research Laboratories led to extensive investigations of the fluorocarbon analogs of the acetylacetonates[6,16,24,29–32]. The most thoroughly studied complexes are those of 1,1,1-trifluoro-2,4-pentanedione and 1,1,1,5,5,5-hexafluoro-2,4-pentanedione, more commonly called trifluoroacetylacetone and hexafluoroacetylacetone. The anions of these ligands, designated *tfa* and *hfa*, respectively, are shown below.

$$CF_3—\overset{\overset{\displaystyle O}{\|}}{C}—CH{=}\overset{\overset{\displaystyle O^-}{|}}{C}—CH_3 \quad tfa$$

$$CF_3—\overset{\overset{\displaystyle O}{\|}}{C}—CH{=}\overset{\overset{\displaystyle O^-}{|}}{C}—CF_3 \quad hfa$$

The studies revealed that chelates of tfa and hfa can be eluted at much lower column temperatures than the corresponding acetyl-acetonates. The trend is most striking and can best be illustrated by citing a few examples. Chromium(III) hexafluoroacetylacet-onate is eluted rapidly at column temperatures as low as 30°C. For chromium(III) acetylacetonate to be eluted in the same time, the column temperature must be well over one hundred degrees higher.

The greater volatility of the fluorocarbon chelates appears to be a general phenomenon[16,33−36]. The reason for this is not clear, but several possible explanations have been advanced. The increase in volatility may be due to a reduction in van der Waals forces and perhaps to a decrease in intermolecular hydrogen bond-ing in the fluorine-containing chelates. Molecular models of octahedral hexafluoroacetylacetonate chelates show that a large portion of the periphery is occupied by the eighteen highly electro-negative fluorine atoms encasing the metal ion in a fluorocarbon shell. The resulting intermolecular attracting forces are weaker than in the unfluorinated complexes. Conceivably the some-what bulkier fluroine atoms could prevent close-packing in the crystal lattice, a factor that should favor greater volatility.

Whatever the cause, the effect is pronounced. Some of the hexafluoroacetylacetonate chelates, e.g. Cr(III), Rh(III), Fe(III), are so volatile that they can be easily steam distilled[30,37]. Most of the complexes rapidly sublime at reduced pressure at temperatures ranging from ambient to 100°C. The significance of such observa-tions is reflected in the gas chromatographic data. Many of the trifluoroacetylacetonates can be eluted at column temperatures between 80 and 150°C and the hexafluoroacetylacetonates at even lower temperatures ranging down to 30°C. This is highly encourag-ing because it means that instead of operating the columns in the temperature range from 150 to 230°C, as is necessary for many of the acetylacetonates, it is possible to operate at lower column temperatures at which thermal decomposition is much less of a problem.

Trifluoroacetylacetonates

A survey study[31] was conducted to determine which of the trifluoroacetylacetonates are sufficiently stable and volatile to be chromatographed.* The selection of a suitable injection port temperature is one of the most difficult and yet critical factors in a survey of this type. The choice must be a compromise between the higher temperatures that will assure rapid and complete vaporization of the less volatile chelates and lower temperatures that will permit temperature-sensitive complexes to be vaporized without decomposing. The temperatures found to be the most suitable turn out to be lower than expected. This may be explained if it is recalled that the complexes are dissolved in a volatile solvent and are consequently already somewhat dispersed. When introduced into the hot injection port the volatile solvent is readily vaporized and the carrier gas dilutes the sample, further facilitating vaporization. When temperature-sensitive species are not present in a sample, it is obviously advantageous to use higher injection port temperatures to make certain that the sample is rapidly vaporized.

The injection port was modified by inserting a glass liner that served two purposes. First, it enabled the operator to check the liner for residue periodically to see whether or not decomposition was occurring or volatilization was incomplete. Secondly, it retarded any reactions that might have occurred between the chelates and the hot metal wall of the injection port and eliminated decomposition that might have been catalyzed by contact with the hot wall.

The results of the study are shown in Table 2.1. The behavior of the complexes can best be described by dividing them into three classes. Class I includes all complexes that were chromatographed successfully without any apparent decomposition either in the injection port or in the column. The chromatograms for these complexes all showed sharp, well-defined peaks with characteristic retention times. Examination of the glass liner in the injection port revealed no residue even after many repetitive runs during several

---

* The survey was conducted under the following conditions: column, borosilicate glass, 4 ft × 4 mm i.d., packed with 0.5 per cent Dow Corning Silicone 710 oil (a phenylmethyl silicone polymer) on silanized glass beads (60–80 mesh); column temperatures, 100–150°C; injection port temperature, 135°C; solvent for samples, benzene; instrument, F and M Model 500 equipped with a thermal conductivity detector cell with W-2 filaments; helium flow rate, 83 ml min^{-1}.

days of operation. Samples of the eluate of all the complexes were collected from the helium stream as it left the detector and examined to ensure that the chelates were eluted intact. For all nine complexes the properties of the eluate matched those of authentic samples.

TABLE 2.1. CHROMATOGRAPHY OF
TRIFLUOROACETYLACETONATE CHELATES[31]

Class I	Class II	Class III
beryllium	iron(III)	neodymium(III)
aluminum	manganese(III)	
gallium(III)[32]	zirconium	
scandium(III)	hafnium	
copper(II)	zinc	
chromium(III)		
vanadium(IV)[38]		
indium(III)		
rhodium(III)		

The Class I complexes are shown in the order of decreasing ease of elution. Retention times were measured at 125°C with the column and conditions described in the footnote. Aluminum trifluoroacetylacetonate was chosen as a standard for calculating relative retention volumes because it is easily prepared and shows excellent elution behavior on columns containing a wide variety of liquid partitioning agents. Relative retention volumes were calculated for the other complexes by dividing their net retention volumes by that of aluminum. The relative retention volumes are: beryllium, 0.35; aluminum, 1.00; gallium(III), 1.8; scandium(III), 2.1; copper(II), 2.5; chromium(III), 2.6; indium(III), 3.0; vanadium(IV) as the vanadyl complex, 3.1; rhodium(III), 5.9. The beryllium and aluminum complexes have unique retention times, indicating that they can be separated and determined in the presence of any of the metals studied with no interferences caused by peak overlapping. Although the relative retention volumes of some of the complexes are very similar, it will be seen in Chapter 3 that by changing the stationary phase and varying the other parameters, one can separate several mixtures of chelates that might appear not to be separable based on retention data obtained for a given type of column under a particular set of conditions.

Because there was no detectable decomposition for any of the metal complexes in Class I, the chromatography of these compounds may be regarded as totally successful. For the compounds in Class II, the chromatographic elutions may be described as successful, but with qualifications. They do produce well-defined peaks with characteristic and reproducible retention times. Samples of the complexes were collected from the eluant stream and identified, verifying that the compounds were eluted intact. However, residue was found in the injection port after experiments with each of the compounds, indicating partial decomposition or incomplete volatilization of the samples. The amount of residue was usually very small, so the extent of decomposition, assuming that to be the source of the residue, was probably slight. If this is true, it is conceivable that one could obtain quantitative data for these chelates provided that the extent of decomposition is constant regardless of the nature of the sample. As noted earlier, caution should be exercised in using such data. $Fe(tfa)_3$ and $Mn(tfa)_3$ are eluted with approximately the same ease as $Cr(tfa)_3$. The hafnium, zirconium, and zinc complexes are eluted much later, with about the same retention times as the rhodium(III) complex. Although chromatographic peaks were obtained for the Class II complexes just as for those in Class I, the appearance of residue in the flash vaporizer chamber makes it necessary as a matter of prudence to treat them as a separate group until their behavior is better defined.

The third class designates compounds that so far have resisted efforts to chromatograph them. Neodymium(JII) trifluoroacetylacetonate is the only complex examined in the survey that fell in this class. At low temperatures the complex remained in the flash vaporizer chamber without volatilizing. As the temperature was increased progressively during successive attempts, thermal decomposition increased. The gas chromatographic signals obtained at higher temperatures were shown to be produced by decomposition products; so efforts to chromatograph this complex were abandoned.

Figure 2.2 shows the separation of a mixture of aluminum,

chromium(III) and rhodium(III) trifluoroacetylacetonates[16]. As will be the case in most of the chromatograms shown, the first peak, which is off-scale, arises from the solvent. The peaks are reasonably well separated but they are much broader than desired. The peaks of compounds with long retention times are much broader than those of the earlier-eluted species. This phenomenon, universally encountered in varying degrees, is undesirable because it is difficult to detect small amounts of the later-eluted complexes.

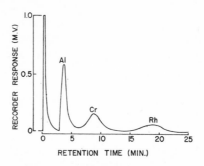

Fig. 2.2. Separation of aluminum, chromium(III) and rhodium(III) trifluoroacetylacetonates[16]. *Sample:* 10 μl. of a mixture of the chelates in CCl_4. *Column temp.:* 150°C. *Column:* borosilicate glass, 4 ft × $\frac{1}{8}$ in. i.d., packed with 0.5 per cent Tergitol NPX on powdered Teflon. *Helium flow rate:* 150 ml min^{-1}.
(Courtesy of *Inorganic Chemistry*)

There are two ways to circumvent this difficulty. The first is to use temperature programming, a technique in which the column temperature is gradually increased during the course of the chromatographic run so as to accelerate the elution of the less volatile components. In this way sharp peaks may be obtained even for the less volatile complexes. The second approach is to make two separate chromatographic runs under isothermal conditions, one at a high column temperature and a second at a lower temperature. At the higher temperature the peaks of the less volatile compounds are much sharper and can be measured more reliably, but the more volatile compounds may be not well separated from each other or from the solvent, thus necessitating the second run at a lower temperature. Both approaches have their advantages, but difficulties in controlling carefully the changing parameters in temperature programming cause the measurements to be less reproducible than those taken under isothermal conditions.

The column used for the chromatogram in Fig. 2.2 contained Tergitol NPX, a polyethoxy nonionic detergent derived from nonylphenol, supported on powdered Teflon. The longer retention times observed and the higher column temperatures required compared to the data shown in the subsequent figures, are caused in part by the polar nature of this partitioning phase. It is usually advisable to avoid polar phases unless they exhibit specificity and can be used to achieve a particularly difficult separation.

The separation of the trifluoroacetylacetonate complexes of beryllium, aluminum and copper(II) is shown in Fig. 2.3. The

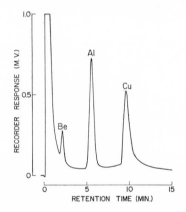

Fig. 2.3. Separation of beryllium, aluminum and copper(II) trifluoroacetylacetonates[31]. *Sample:* 4 μl. of a benzene soln. of the chelates. *Column temp.:* programmed from 100 to 130°C at 3° min⁻¹. *Injection port temp.:* 135°C. *Detector block temp.:* 150°C. *Column:* borosilicate glass, 4 ft × 4 mm i.d., packed with 0.5 per cent Dow Corning Silicone 710 oil on silanized glass microbands (60–70 mesh). *Helium flow rate:* 83 ml min⁻¹. *Instrument:* F and M Model 500, thermal conductivity detector with W-2 filaments.
(Courtesy of the *American Chemical Society*)

column temperature was initially 100°C and was programmed to 130°C at three degrees per minute. The sample contained 0.15 μg of beryllium, 2.2 μg of aluminum and 11.7 μg of copper. The chromatogram shows that microgram and sub-microgram quantities can easily be measured with a conventional thermal conductivity detector cell. The peaks are sharp and the compounds have relatively short retention times even at the modest column temperatures employed. $Al(tfa)_3$ and $Cu(tfa)_2$ recently have been found to form quantitatively and be readily extracted from aqueous solutions with non-aqueous solvents[39] (see Chapter 4). It is anticipated that there will be little difficulty in finding conditions that will permit the extraction of the beryllium complex as well. This, then, provides a basis for the simultaneous determination of these three metals.

The separation of aluminum and scandium is depicted in Fig. 2.4. The compounds are separated cleanly and rapidly when the column is operated isothermally at 125°C.

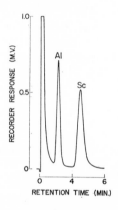

FIG. 2.4. Separation of aluminum and scandium(III) trifluoro-acetylacetonates[31], *Sample:* 1.5 μl. of a benzene solution of the chelates. *Column temp.:* 125°C. Same column and other conditions as in Fig. 2.3.
(Courtesy of the *American Chemical Society*)

In Fig. 2.5 the chromatographic separation of a mixture of five metals is shown. The sample contained 0.38 μg of beryllium, 2.22 μg of aluminum, 2.40 μg of scandium, 8.00 μg of indium and 2.44 μg of rhodium. Beryllium is eluted first, followed by aluminum, scandium, indium and rhodium. The separation of the five metals requires only fifteen minutes. It should also be stressed that the experimental manipulations required to accomplish such a separation are virtually effortless in comparison to most other procedures. To make a chromatographic run it is necessary only to take an aliquot with a microsyringe, inject the sample into the carrier gas stream, and activate a switch to start the automatic temperature programming controller. These operations require only a few seconds, and nothing more need be done until it is time to inject another sample.

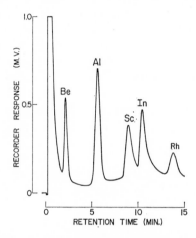

FIG. 2.5. Separation of beryllium, aluminum, scandium(III), indium(III) and rhodium(III) trifluoroacetylacetonates[31]. *Sample:* 4 μl. of a mixture of the chelates in benzene. *Column temp.:* programmed from 100 to 135°C at 3° min⁻¹. Same column and other conditions as in Fig. 2.3.
(Courtesy of the *American Chemical Society*)

The chromatogram shows that scandium is well separated from beryllium and aluminum. This is significant because beryllium and aluminum are often found with scandium in rare earth ores, and the chromatogram indicates that it is possible to separate the trio easily. Thorium and the lanthanides also appear frequently with scandium; so it was of interest to ascertain whether they produce chromatographic peaks that would interfere with that of scandium. Under the conditions shown in Fig. 2.5 there was no interference by the complex of thorium or that of a representative lanthanide, neodymium(III).

There are probably few elements that have caused the analytical chemist more difficulties than scandium. It is prone to occur with a number of other elements exhibiting similar chemical properties, making its quantitative isolation very difficult to accomplish. In the light of these difficulties the application of gas chromatography would seem to offer great promise. A principal forte of gas chromatography is its ability to separate chemically similar species. Chemical similarity poses few obstacles because the separation depends only on small differences in the volatility and the solubility of the complexes in the liquid partitioning agent. This has made possible the separation of a number of mixtures that are difficult to separate by other methods. The facile separation of mixtures of beryllium, aluminum, gallium and indium trifluoroacetylaceto-nates and the chloro-hexafluoroacetylacetonato complexes of titanium, tantalum and niobium are excellent illustrations[6,32] (see Chapter 4).

Up to this point most of the emphasis has been on complete and quantitative separation and analysis, but we should not neglect the less elegant, yet potentially important, possibilities of qualitative and semi-quantitative analyses. When only a rough idea of the sample composition is desired, one can sacrifice component resolution for speed. Figure 2.6 shows a rapid scan of a mixture containing six metals: beryllium, aluminum, gallium(III), chromium(III), indium(III) and rhodium(III). The amounts of metal ranged from 0.05 μg of beryllium to 2.7 μg of chromium. All of the metals except indium produce distinct peaks with characteristic and readily identifiable retention times. Indium appears as a barely discernible but reproducible shoulder on the sixth peak. The scan requires only eight minutes and, in addition to establishing the qualitative presence of each of the six metals, it provides a very rough estimate of relative abundance. The curious appearance of two peaks for the chromium complex can be accounted for by recalling that in octahedral complexes unsymmetrical bidentate ligands may give rise to two geometrical isomers. The *trans* isomer is eluted first and the more polar *cis* isomer follows[16] (see Chapter 5).

For qualitative identification purposes it is possible to work even with compounds that show marked decomposition, so long as a measurable quantity of the complex is eluted intact. This is practical because the decomposition products are usually formed over a time span and therefore are not generally eluted as sharp and distinct peaks but, instead, cause the baseline to drift slowly and to be higher than normal. The result is a sharp, clearly recognizable peak superimposed on a baseline showing gradual seemingly random undulations, an admittedly undesirable form of data presentation, but of value, nonetheless.

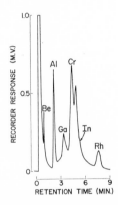

Fig. 2.6. Qualitative analysis of a mixture of beryllium, aluminum, gallium(III), chromium(III), indium(III) and rhodium (III) trifluoroacetylacetonates[31]. *Sample:* 1 μl. of a mixture of the chelates in benzene. *Column temp.:* 125°C. *Injection port temp.:* 140°C. *Detector block temp.:* 162°C. *Column:* borosilicate glass, 4 ft × 4 mm i.d., packed with 5 per cent Dow Corning High Vacuum Silicone grease on Chromosorb W (30–60 mesh). *Helium flow rate:* 83 ml min⁻¹.
(Courtesy of the *American Chemical Society*)

The chromatograms shown so far have been for mixtures in which the amounts of each of the components are present in approximately the same order of magnitude. But it is also important to know whether one metal can be separated and measured in the presence of much larger amounts of another without a prior step to remove the major constituent. Figure 2.7 shows the separation of 0.0059 μg of beryllium in the presence of 2000 times as much aluminum[31]. The beryllium peak appears as a small but unmistakably distinct peak just after the solvent. After the beryllium was eluted the signal to the recorder was attenuated by a factor of eight in order to keep the aluminum peak on-scale. The analysis was complete in five minutes and showed that major and minor components can easily be recorded during the same chromatographic run. The order in which the compounds are eluted

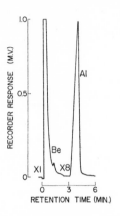

FIG. 2.7. Separation of major and minor constituents[31]. *Sample:* 2 μl of benzene solution of the beryllium and aluminum trifluoroacetylacetonates. The sample contained 0.0059 μg of Be and 11.2 μg of Al. *Column temp.:* 115°C. Other conditions same as in Fig. 2.6.
(Courtesy of the *American Chemical Society*)

is important, however. It is much easier to detect minor constituents when they appear early in the chromatographic run. If a minor constituent follows a major one, the signal may be swamped if the compounds are not well separated. If this proves troublesome, and conditions cannot be found under which the separation is improved sufficiently, it may be necessary to search for a stationary phase that will selectively retard the major component so as to reverse the order of elution. Also it may be advisable to select a solvent that is eluted after the trace constituent so as to eliminate any interference caused by the solvent. This allows use of operating conditions that will give shorter retention times, in turn yielding sharper peaks with accompanying enhancement of sensitivity. Ross and Wheeler[1,2] have taken excellent advantage of this approach in ultra-trace determinations.

In Fig. 2.7 the skewed appearance of the aluminum peak (so called "leading", as opposed to the more common undesirable phenomenon "tailing") indicates that the column was overloaded. The overloading was not serious, however, for the peak is still reasonably sharp. This deviation from ideality can be counteracted by increasing the percentage of the liquid phase, increasing the column temperature, or reducing the sample size.

The effect on the retention times of the complexes caused by varying the column temperature can be seen by comparing Figs. 2.6 and 2.7. A ten degree drop almost doubles the retention times. This is a general phenomenon not limited to beryllium and aluminum, and provides the easiest and most practical means of altering the elution behavior.

Investigators in other laboratories have also recently reported separating mixtures of trifluoroacetylacetonates[21,40]. The separation of the beryllium, aluminum and chromium(III) chelates is shown in Fig. 2.8. The shorter retention times compared with those in Fig. 2.7 can be explained in part by the shorter column length.

Quantitative studies on the trifluoroacetylacetonates are described in detail in Chapter 4 and are summarized as follows. Hill and Gesser[21] have reported a quantitative study on mixtures of the beryllium, aluminum and chromium(III) chelates based on the chromatogram shown in Fig. 2.8. Mixtures of beryllium, aluminum, gallium and indium were studied by Schwarberg and co-workers[6,32], who reported that any mixture of these chelates can be separated and determined quickly and reliably. The relative mean error for the analysis of mixtures of the complexes was 2 per cent. The success of the quantitative investigations and the encouragement offered by the stability data summarized in Table 2.1 make it clear that the trifluoroacetylacetonates provide fertile ground for many future studies. Chelates of fourteen metal ions have been chromatographed successfully and the list continues to grow.

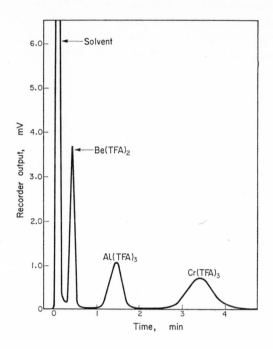

FIG. 2.8. Separation of beryllium, aluminum and chromium(III) trifluoroacetylacetonates[21]. *Sample:* 1 μl. of a carbon tetrachloride solution of the chelates. *Column temp.:* 106°C. *Column:* copper tubing, 0.06 in. i.d., 1 ft long, packed with 7.5 per cent SE-30 silicone gum rubber on 40–60 mesh firebrick. *Nitrogen flow rate:* 30 ml min⁻¹. Flame ionization detector. (Courtesy of *Journal of Gas Chromatography*)

Hexafluoroacetylacetonates

The chromatography of hexafluoroacetylacetonates was first studied by Sievers, Ponder, Morris and Moshier[16], who found this class to be more readily eluted than any of the others yet examined. The extraordinary volatility and the ease with which they are eluted can be seen by referring to Fig. 2.9. The column was operated only slightly above room temperature; yet the vapor pressures of the chelates are high enough to permit movement through the column.* With so low a column temperature, thermal degradation is no longer a concern.

Aluminum, beryllium, and iron(III) hexafluoroacetylacetonates can also be chromatographed at low column temperatures. The separation of the aluminum and chromium(III) complexes is

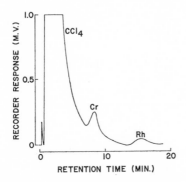

Fig. 2.9. Separation of chromium(III) and rhodium(III) hexafluoroacetylacetonates[16]. *Sample:* 10 μl. of a mixture of the chelates in CCl_4. *Column temp.:* 30°C. *Column:* borosilicate glass, 4 ft × ⅛ in. i.d., packed with 0.5 per cent D. C. silicone grease on glass microbeads (60–80 mesh). *Helium flow rate:* 80 ml min⁻¹. The first peak is caused by a small amount of air unavoidably introduced when the sample was injected.

shown in Fig. 2.10[1]. The solvent, toluene, produced no peak because the electron capture detector is insensitive to hydrocarbons. The third peak in the chromatogram was caused by a trace of an electron-capturing impurity in the solvent. The retention time of toluene was determined in an independent experiment to be six minutes. This is quite surprising because it means that both complexes have shorter retention times than toluene. It was also shown that the complexes are eluted more rapidly than chloroform[41] ,which is further indicative of the extraordinary volatility of the hexafluoroacetylacetonates.

Juvet and Durbin, in their studies of detector selectivity, worked with mixtures of chromium(III) iron(III) and rhodium(III)

* Fractions of the eluate were collected and examined by ultraviolet spectroscopy to verify that the complexes were eluted.

hexafluoroacetylacetonates[3]. They deliberately chose conditions under which the chelates were poorly separated in order to demonstrate the selectivity of the flame photometric detector (see Chapter 3). The column temperatures found to be adequate to produce

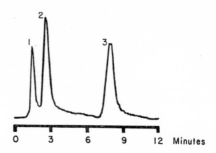

FIG. 2.10.   Separation of aluminum and chromium(III) hexafluoroacetylacetonates[1].   *Sample:* A toluene solution of a mixture of the chelates.   *Column temp.:* 65°C.   *Column:* 11 ft × ⅛ in. o.d., stainless steel, packed with 20 per cent. D. C. Silicone 710R on Gas Chrom Z. Electron capture detector. *Carrier gas.:* nitrogen.   Peak 1, Al(hfa)₃; peak 2, Cr(hfa)₃; peak 3, impurity in the solvent.
(Courtesy of *Analytical Chemistry*)

retention times under five minutes were between sixty and seventy degrees centigrade.   On a column with 5 per cent Dow Corning Silicone 200 (dimethylpolysiloxane) on silanized Chromosorb W, the chromium complex was eluted first, followed by the iron, and then the rhodium.   Other workers[21] have separated mixtures of the beryllium, aluminum and chromium(III) hexafluoroacetylacetonates, as shown in Fig. 2.11 (see Chapter 4).

Experience has shown that the sublimation behavior of complexes often gives a good indication of whether the compounds are sufficiently volatile to permit chromatography.   Generally speaking, if a compound sublimes rapidly at 0.05 mm at temperatures not so high as to cause decomposition, gas chromatographic elution is practicable.   This takes into account only the volatility requirement, of course; so such potential problems as solvolysis in the column may still be encountered.   Nevertheless, sublimation data are of value because they indicate the probability of success under the most ideal conditions. If the data indicate that a compound is sufficiently volatile and thermally stable to permit gas phase transport, should chromatography of the compound fail, the worker is stimulated to try other column packing materials and temperature and flow conditions. On the other hand, if the data indicate that the compounds are non-volatile or thermally unstable, further experimentation is useless.

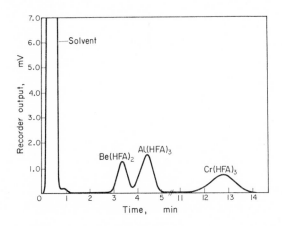

FIG. 2.11. Separation of beryllium, aluminum and chromium(III) hexafluoroacetylacetonates[21]. *Sample:* 1 μl. of a carbon tetrachloride solution containing 16.5 μg Be(hfa)₂, 25.1 μg Al(hfa)₃ and 18.0 μg Cr(hfa)₃. *Column temp.:* 50°C. *Column:* 5 ft × 0.06 in. i.d., containing 7.5 per cent SE-30 on 40–60 mesh firebrick.
(Courtesy of *Journal of Gas Chromatography*)

The hexafluoroacetylacetonates of manganese(II), iron(II), cobalt(II), nickel(II) and copper(II) sublime rapidly at 0.05 mm at temperatures between 50 and 70°C. The thorium(IV) and neodymium(III) complexes sublime slowly at 100°C/0.05 mm. This taken alone would indicate a good chance of success in chromatographing the complexes, but there is a possible complication. Of the group, all the compounds except that of thorium occur as hydrates[42]. The effect of coordinated water groups on the behavior of the compounds in a chromatographic column is not yet known. There may be no deleterious effects, but polymerization via olation, and dissociation of the coordinated water during the elution are distinct possibilities.

The successful sublimation of neodymium(III) hexafluoroacetylacetonate offers some hope for using gas chromatography in the separation of the lanthanides. For many years chemists have sought methods for separating the rare earths and, more particularly, the lanthanides, based on differences in the presumed volatility of certain rare earth compounds. Unfortunately, early statements regarding the volatility of the tris (pentane-2,4-dionato)-lanthanides have proven incorrect[43]. Brimm[44] examined some of the earlier claims and reported that the complexes possess only very slight volatility and that they cannot be separated on this basis owing to thermal instability. To complicate matters, the lanthanides may form complexes with coordination numbers higher than six. Tetrakis complexes with bidentate ligands are sometimes obtained and the identities of the molecular species in the different physical states are often in question. Even though the tetrakis complexes of β-diketonato-lanthanides carry a formal uninegative charge there is some evidence that they, as well as the neutral tris complexes, may be sufficiently volatile to be useful in gas chromatography. For example, triethylammonium tetrakis (1,1,1,5,5,5-hexafluoro-2,4-pentanedionato)europate(III) was recovered unchanged after sublimation at 115–117°C (0.05–0.1 mm)[45]. The emission spectra of the original compound, the sublimate and the residue were identical. As more is learned about the factors affecting volatility, it seems only a matter of time before it will be possible to separate the lanthanides by gas chromatography.

For some of the metals in groups IVB, VB and VIB, certain mixed complexes containing both chloro groups and hexafluoroacetylacetonato moieties have been shown to be quite volatile and easily chromatographed[6]. In aqueous solutions hydrolysis of such species as titanium(IV), niobium(V) and tantalum(V) is an ever-present problem. For this reason a new sample preparation route that would not involve working in aqueous solutions was sought. One promising procedure is to convert a mixture of oxides to the anhydrous chlorides, followed by reaction of the chlorides with the ligand. As mentioned in an earlier section carbon tetra-chloride can be used in sealed tube reactions to convert oxides or sulfides to the chlorides. To the chlorides, dissolved or suspended in carbon tetrachloride, the ligand is added, and hydrogen chloride evolves. Usually no buffering or neutralization is required. The complex will be a completely or partially chelated species, depend-ing on the oxidation state and coordination number of the metal. Ideally one would like the coordination number to be exactly twice the charge on the metal ion. In such cases, if univalent bidentate ligands are used, completely chelated species will generally result. The reaction of aluminum chloride with hexafluoroacetyl-acetone, for example, yields the completely chelated $Al(hfa)_3$[30,46]. With titanium(IV) chloride, however, an incompletely chelated compound results[6].

$$TiCl_4 + 2H(hfa) \rightarrow TiCl_2(hfa)_2 + 2HCl$$

For complete substitution and chelation to occur, the metal would have to accommodate eight oxygen donors. Although a coordina-tion number of eight is not unknown for titanium(IV), it is rarely encountered. The reactions of niobium(V) and tantalum(V) chlorides also yield mixed-ligand chloro-hexafluoroacetylacetonato complexes[6]. These complexes are susceptible to hydrolysis by atmospheric moisture. Special handling procedures must be used, but the ease with which difficult separations can be achieved warrants the extra precautions. The separation of titanium(IV), niobium(V), and tantalum(V) chloro-hexafluoroacetylacetonates is discussed in Chapter 4. It will be observed that the mixed-ligand complexes of niobium and tantalum are much more volatile and yield far better chromatograms than the parent chlorides[6,56].

The hexafluoroacetylacetonates derive their greatest significance from the unusually low column temperatures that can be used in their chromatography. This advantage may be partially offset, however, by the peculiar behavior of the ligand in aqueous solu-tion. In the presence of water, hexafluoroacetylacetone reacts to give 1,1,1,5,5,5-hexafluoro-2,2,4,4-tetrahydroxypentane[48,49]. To what extent this behavior will be troublesome in solvent extraction or other sample preparation procedures has not been established. In contrast, trifluoroacetylacetone shows no tendency to react with water to form the analogous tetrahydroxy compound; so no difficulties of this type are anticipated.

Other Fluorocarbon β-diketonates

In the search for other volatile fluorocarbon chelates, two alterations in the hexafluoroacetylacetonato moiety have been investigated[50]. One approach was to replace one of the two protons on the 3-position in hexafluoroacetylacetone. With this ligand, 1,1,1,3,5,5,5-heptafluoro-2,4-pentanedione, the only proton remaining would be displaced upon complex formation, and one would obtain totally fluorinated chelates.

The second approach was to substitute higher fluoroalkyl groups in place of one or both of the trifluoromethyl groups. Accordingly, studies of 1,1,1,5,5,6,6,7,7,7-decafluoro-2,4-heptanedione and 1,1,1,5,5,6,6,6-octafluoro-2,4-hexanedione were undertaken. The structures and abbreviations of the ligands are shown below.

$$O \cdots H \cdots O$$
$$CF_3CF_2CF_2—C^{\cdots}CH^{\cdots}C—CF_3 \quad H(dfhd)$$

$$O \cdots H \cdots O$$
$$CF_3CF_2—C^{\cdots}CH^{\cdots}C—CF_3 \quad H(ofhd)$$

$Cr(ofhd)_3$, $Cr(dfhd)_3$, $Zr(dfhd)_4$ and $Hf(dfhd)_4$, all liquids at room temperature, can be distilled in a molecular still at 60°C/0.02 mm[50]. Of possible importance is the volatility of the magnesium and calcium complexes of H(dfhd). They sublime at 135°C/0.005 mm and 100°C/0.003 mm, respectively. If they prove to be stable to solvolysis in a column, gas chromatographic analysis of the alkaline earths may be possible.

An effort was made to determine the influence of various substituents on the ease of elution of a series of chromium(III) complexes. Table 2.2 shows the results. Though it is not safe to draw any sweeping conclusions, certain trends are evident. Chromium(III) benzoylacetonate was not sufficiently volatile to be vaporized and eluted under the same conditions as chromium(III) acetylacetonate. Chromium(III) trifluoroacetylacetonate was eluted at substantially lower temperatures, and the other complexes at even lower temperatures. The relative ease of elution is seen to increase as follows: $Cr(acac)_3 < < Cr(tfa)_3 < < Cr(dfhd)_3 < Cr(ofhd)_3 < Cr(hfa)_3$.

TABLE 2.2. COMPARATIVE ELUTION BEHAVIOR OF
CHROMIUM(III) CHELATES[38]

R_1	R_2	Col. temp. °C	Retention time (min)	
C_6H_5	CH_3	148	–*	
CH_3	CH_3	148	5.3	
CF_3	CH_3	148	1.0	
CF_3	CH_3	105	8.6†	
CF_3	C_3F_7	60	5.7	increasing
CF_3	C_2F_5	60	2.4	ease of
CF_3	CF_3	60	1.7	↓ elution

Column: same as Fig. 2.6; *Helium flow rate:* 86 ml min⁻¹. Detector block temp., 165°C; injection port temperature, 135°C.
　* Not sufficiently volatile to be vaporized at the temp. of the injection port.
　† For complexes with unsymmetrical ligands, the retention time of the *trans* isomer is shown in instances when the isomers were well enough separated to permit assignment.

Other Metal Chelates

A limited number of other classes of chelates appear to be sufficiently volatile to generate interest. The complexes of 2,2,6,6-tetramethyl-3,5-heptanedione (more commonly called dipivaloylmethane) are prominent examples. Several of the complexes are known to be volatile[51,52], but perhaps the most intriguing are those of the alkali metals. The lithium, sodium, and potassium complexes sublime at reduced pressure, suggesting that gas chromatographic separation of even the alkali metals may be feasible. The magnesium, cobalt(II), nickel(II), zinc(II), chromium(III), manganese(III) and cobalt(III) complexes also sublime at reduced pressure.

In turning from the β-diketonates to chelates containing nitrogen donors, we find a few compounds that are somewhat less volatile than those discussed previously but are interesting owing to their unusual thermal stability. Charles and Langer[53] have shown that the 8-hydroxyquinolate complexes of copper(II), lead(II), nickel(II), zinc, gallium, aluminum, indium, iron(III), chromium(III), cobalt(II), cadmium(II), manganese(II) and magnesium sublime *in vacuo* at temperatures between 250 and 500°C. They sublimed 50 mg samples and found only traces of residue (less than 0.5 mg), showing that decomposition was negligible. Even though the compounds are thermally stable, their chromatography will not be as straightforward as that of more volatile compounds because of the problems encountered in operating at high temperatures. Suitable liquid partitioning agents for high temperature gas chromatography are few in number. Column bleeding and reactivity of the column packing materials towards the compounds being chromatographed become acute at high temperatures; furthermore the choice of detectors is rather limited.

Klesper, Corwin and Turner[54] have chromatographed mixtures of porphyrins under rather unusual conditions. In attempts to chromatograph porphyrins by conventional gas chromatography, sufficiently high vapor pressures were reached only at temperatures where decomposition occurred. They were able to overcome this difficulty by using high pressure gas chromatography and operating above the critical temperature of the carrier gas. A mixture of 1 mg of nickel etioporphyrin II and 1 mg of nickel mesoporphyrin IX dimethylester dissolved in 0.2 ml *o*-dichlorobenzene was introduced into a column packed with 33 per cent polyethyleneglycol on Chromosorb W. Dichlorodifluoromethane was the carrier gas, and the flow rate varied from 50–150 ml min^{-1}. The pressure in the column was initially 1830 psi. After one hour of operation a separated band of nickel etioporphyrin II was located eight inches from the beginning of the column, and a band of nickel porphyrin

IX dimethylester was located three inches from the beginning. X-ray powder patterns proved that the components were unchanged, and recovery was nearly quantitative. Although high pressure chromatography may find important application in highly specialized separations, experimental inconveniences make it unattractive for general use.

The discussion in the foregoing sections is summarized in Table 2.3. The table is not intended to be exhaustive but only to indicate

TABLE 2.3. GAS CHROMATOGRAPHY OF METAL CHELATES

Li piv*	Be tfa*** hfa*** acac***														
Na piv*	Mg dfhd*											Al tfa*** hfa*** acac***			
K piv*	Ca dfhd*	Sc tfa*** acac	Ti(IV) hfa***	V(IV) tfa***	Cr(III) tfa*** hfa*** acac***	Mn(III) tfa**	Fe(III) tfa** hfa	Co(II) hfa* piv*	Ni(II) hfa* piv*	Cu(II) tfa*** acac. hfa	Zn tfa** hfa* piv*	Ga tfa***	Ge		
Rb	Sr	Y	Zr tfa** dfhd*	Nb hfa**	Mo	Tc	Ru	Rh(III) tfa*** hfa***	Pd	Ag	Cd	In tfa***	Sn	Sb
Cs	Ba	LANTHANIDES hfa*	Hf tfa** dfhd*	Ta hfa**	W	Re	Os	Ir	Pt	Au	Hg	Tl tfa	Pb	Bi
Fr	Ra	ACTINIDES Th-tfa*												

* Complexes suspected to be sufficiently volatile to be chromatographed.
** Complexes whose elution has been confirmed but with evidence of slight decomposition.
*** Complexes that can be eluted without evidence of decomposition.
tfa = trifluoroacetylacetonate.
hfa = hexafluoroacetylacetonate.
acac = acetylacetonate.
dfhd = decafluoroheptanedionate.
piv = dipivaloylmethanate.

the types of complexes that appear at this time to show the greatest promise from an analytical standpoint. Undoubtedly many other types of compounds will eventually find use in metal analysis by gas chromatography.

Metal Halides

A number of metal halides are volatile and can be chromato-graphed in the gas phase. In the earlier work, Freiser[47] reported the separation of tin(IV) chloride and titanium(IV) chloride on a column containing n-hexadecane, and Juvet and Wachi[55] described the separation of antimony(III) chloride and titanium(IV) chloride with a fused salt stationary phase. (See Fig. 2.12.)

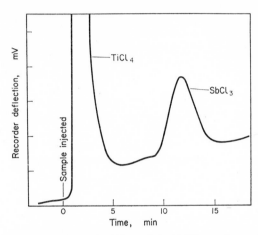

FIG. 2.12. Separation of TiCl$_4$ and SbCl$_3$[55]. *Column:* boro-silicate glass, 12 ft × 6 mm o.d., containing BiCl$_3$–PbCl$_2$ eutectic mixture on C-22 firebrick. *Column temp.:* 240°C. (Courtesy of *Analytical Chemistry*)

Several metal chlorides have boiling points under 350°C, as seen in Table 2.4. The gas chromatographic behavior of about half of the compounds listed has been studied[10,11,47,55-61].

Chemists seeking to devise new methods of analysis, as opposed to those interested in the separation of the chlorides *per se*, will view the chlorides with mixed feelings, The volatility of some chlorides, especially those of the amphoteric elements, will make possible the analysis of elements otherwise not accessible. For this reason the chlorides merit thorough examination. On the other hand, the compounds are far from ideal in several respects. The literature is filled with reports of difficulties arising from the reactivity of the metal halides[10,11,55-60,62]. The halides are easily hydrolyzed by atmospheric moisture, necessitating special sample introduction techniques such as enclosing the injection port in a dry box. Special precautions must be taken to eliminate traces of moisture from the carrier gas. In the column, at elevated temperatures the halides react with many liquid partitioning phases, severely limiting the choice of materials with which the column can be packed. Metallic surfaces throughout the flow system are also often

TABLE 2.4. BOILING POINTS OF METAL CHLORIDES[56]

Metal	B.P., °C	Metal	B.P., °C
Boron(III)	12.5	Antimony(III)	222.3
Silicon(IV)	57.6	Niobium(V)	240.5
Germanium(IV)	83.1	Tantalum(V)	242
Tin(IV)	114.1	Gold(III)	265 (sub.)
Arsenic(III)	130.2	Molybdenum(V)	258
Titanium(IV)	136.4	Tungsten(V)	275.6
Antimony(V)	140.0	Zirconium(IV)	300 (sub.)
Vanadium(IV)	149.5	Mercury(II)	302
Aluminum(III)	177.8 (sub.)	Iron(III)	315
Gallium(III)	201.2	Tungsten(VI)	346.7

attacked. Even in instances when reactivity does not seem to be a problem, the chromatographic peaks are often broad and poorly defined. Figure 2.13 is illustrative of some of the difficulties encountered. It will be noted that the peaks are very broad and have spurious shoulders. Clearly, the usefulness of compounds exhibiting such poor chromatographic behavior is quite limited.

Fortunately some of the halides give better chromatograms. The work with uranium hexafluoride[62-64] represents a triumph in technique over the problems associated with chromatographing highly reactive halogen compounds. In this work the chromatography of uranium hexafluoride, chlorine, chlorine trifluoride, chlorine monofluoride, hydrogen fluoride, perchloryl fluoride, fluorine, fluorine monoxide, chlorine monoxide, chlorine dioxide, and perfluoromethylcyclohexane was studied. It was necessary to construct the entire flow system of unusually non-reactive materials. The inert solid supports were powdered polytetrafluoroethylene and polytrifluoromonochloroethylene, and the stationary phases were Kel-F oils (polytrifluoromonochloroethylene). Specially constructed sample introduction systems and detectors were required. This work demonstrates that if one is willing to make extensive modifications in equipment and technique, it is possible to chromatograph even highly reactive compounds. As the experimental difficulties associated with high temperature chromatography of reactive compounds are overcome, the use of halides in metal analysis probably will become more attractive.

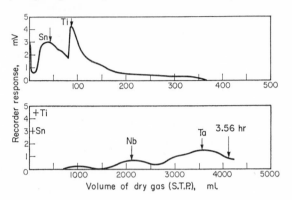

FIG. 2.13. Chromatography of tin(IV), titanium(IV), niobium(V) and tantalum(V) chlorides[56]. *Column:* Copper tubing, 1.6 m × 0.25 in. o.d., packed with 34.4 per cent squalane on Red Chromosorb (30–60 mesh). *Column temp.:* 200°C. *Helium flow rate:* 40.2 ml min⁻¹. The volume scale and flow rate is for ml. of dry gas at 1 atm and 0°C corrected for the pressure drop.
(Courtesy of *Journal of Chromatography*)

The chromatography of germanium(IV), arsenic(III), iron(III), mercury(II), and tin(IV) chlorides has recently been examined by Tadmor[10,11,60]. He found that germanium(IV) and arsenic(III) chlorides give well-defined peaks by gas–solid chromatography on Sil-O-Cel fire brick, but in gas–liquid experiments the chlorides reacted with the silicone grease stationary phase. Mercury(II) and iron(III) chlorides were partially separated using a molten bismuth chloride liquid phase on Sil-O-Cel brick at 290°C. Although the peaks were sharp and no spurious signals appeared, recovery of some of the compounds from the effluent stream was incomplete. The separation of a mixture of tin(IV) chloride, tin(IV) bromide and tin(IV) iodide on a Sil-O-Cel column coated with aluminum bromide was also recently claimed[60].

Boron trichloride was studied by Myers and Putnam[57], who sought analytical procedures that could be used for separating the components of samples obtained from diborane and chloroborane syntheses. Column temperatures between −78 and 40°C were used in the separation of boron trichloride from diborane, dichloroborane, monochloroborane and hydrogen chloride. Zado[58] has attempted to develop a method for the trace analysis of boron in graphite by gas chromatography of boron trichloride. In preliminary experiments a one-gram sample of nuclear graphite thoroughly mixed with 0.005 g of sodium fluoride was heated slowly to 1500–1600°C and the temperature was then raised to 2800°C. A stream of nitrogen saturated with dry carbon tetrachloride vapor was passed over the sample so that boron trichloride was formed, and the gaseous reaction products were trapped in a liquid oxygen cooled U-tube filled with quartz wool. The condensate was then vaporized and fed into a gas chromatography column. The glass column, 200 cm × 4 mm i.d., was filled with fluorocarbon oil coated on kieselguhr and was maintained at 25°C. Phosgene, chlorine, and hydrogen chloride were eluted first, followed by boron trichloride and finally carbon tetrachloride. The boron trichloride peak was diffuse and exhibited considerable tailing. With a thermal conductivity detector, the lower limit of detectability of boron in graphite was found to be 2 ppm. With the more sensitive electron capture detector it is expected that a much lower level of detectability will be achieved.

One important non-analytical application of gas chromatography is ultrapurification. The potential of the technique has been discussed in detail[65,66] but relatively little experimental work has yet been described. Special attention was given to the purification of tellurium(II) and arsenic(III) chlorides, and the use of fused salt stationary phases was recommended. In order to reduce the possibilities of contamination or reaction, a fused salt with the same anion as the compound being chromatographed should be employed.

Vlasov, Sychev and Lapitskii[61] have demonstrated that gas–solid chromatography can be used in purifying titanium(IV) chloride. Titanium(IV) chloride containing 5 per cent iron(III) chloride was purified in ten- to fifteen-gram quantities by passing it through a column packed with silica gel that had been washed with HCl and treated with chlorine gas at 350°C for 20 hr. Dry chlorine gas was the carrier and the column was maintained at 380°C. Titanium tetrachloride was collected in glass receivers within one to two minutes after injection. Iron(III) chloride was retained on the column, and the titanium(IV) chloride collected contained less than 5×10^{-8} per cent iron.

CHEMICAL AND PHYSICAL PROPERTIES OF FLUOROCARBON β-DIKETONATE CHELATES

Many studies have been conducted and much has been written on the chemistry of the metal acetylacetonates. The classical work of Morgan and his collaborators and contemporaries[67] greatly improved our understanding of this interesting class of compounds. For many, it is a great temptation to dismiss the chemistry of the fluorocarbon chelates as being strictly analogous to that of the acetylacetonates. It is true that in many ways their behaviors and structures are similar, but there are some important differences, particularly in the methods that can be used for their syntheses. In the following a survey of the studies that have been made on the fluorocarbon β-diketonate chelates is given.

Ligand Behavior and Synthesis of the Metal Complexes

Trifluoroacetylacetone can be prepared by condensation of acetone and ethyl trifluoroacetate with sodium ethoxide.*[33,36] Reid and Calvin[68] recommended modifications that eliminate the necessity for forming the copper complex in the purification procedure. The ligand boils at 107°C[33], is soluble in most common organic solvents, and its refractive index is 1.3864 at

---

* Trifluoroacetylacetone and hexafluoroacetylacetone are also available from commercial sources (e.g. Columbia Organic Chemicals Co., Columbia, South Carolina, and Peninsular Chem Research, Inc., Gainesville, Florida). It has been observed that the purity of most commerical samples is poor; so they should be purified by fractional distillation before use.

25°C measured at the sodium D line[39]. Its solubility in water is markedly pH dependent, increasing as the pH is raised. The distribution of the ligand between chloroform and water in mixtures of the two as employed in solvent extraction has been measured as a function of pH[39]. The distribution ratio (concentration in chloroform/concentration in water) decreases from 2.39 at pH 0.17 to 0.15 at pH 7.78. Equilibrium is reached within five minutes in experiments in which the ligand is initially in the chloroform layer. Distribution coefficients between benzene and dilute hydrochloric acid solutions have also been reported[69].

Trifluoroacetylacetone reacts with ammonia in solution[36] and in the gas phase[70] to form the ammonium salt. Ammonium trifluoroacetylacetonate can be synthesized in excellent yield by bubbling dry nitrogen through a sample of the ligand and passing the vapor stream into a vessel in which an excess of gaseous ammonia is maintained[70].* The ammonium salt is an easily sublimed white solid; samples left in open containers are rapidly lost to the atmosphere. The salt is soluble in water, acetone, ethanol and methanol, but insoluble in carbon tetrachloride and chloroform. It is reasonably stable in the solid state for short periods of time, but on storing for several days it gradually decomposes to a yellow oil. Freshly prepared aqueous or alcoholic solutions of the ammonium salt can be used to synthesize many of the metal complexes by simple metathesis with nitrate or chloride metal salts. Illustratively, mixtures of aqeous solutions of the ammonium salt and cupric chloride yield copper(II) trifluoroacetylacetonate. The ammonium salt formed *in situ* is a useful intermediate in some syntheses; e.g. the method described by Young[71] for the synthesis of aluminum acetylacetonate from aqueous ammoniacal solutions of acetylacetone works well for preparing aluminum trifluoroacetylacetonate. A note of caution should be injected at this point, however. Aqueous solutions of ammonium trifluoroacetylacetonate are very unstable and decompose in a matter of hours; therefore they must always be prepared just before use[70].

---

* A porous, loosely-fitting plug of glass wool should be inserted in the unused neck of the flask to reduce loss of the flocculent product.

Van Uitert, Fernelius and Douglas[72] have found that dioxane-water solutions of trifluoroacetylacetone are unstable. They noted anomalies in the pH curves when titrating with base in determining the acid dissociation constant of the ligand. The anomalies were attributed to hydrolysis, but self-condensation or any reaction consuming the ligand could also produce the discrepancies. Hexafluoroacetylacetone shows no tendency to decompose under the same conditions. The acid dissociation constants in 74.5 per cent dioxane–water solutions were found to decrease with increasing fluorine substitution. The constants are 12.7 for acetylacetone, 8.7 for trifluoroacetylacetone, and 6.0 for hexafluoroacetylacetone, showing the marked effect of the strongly electron-withdrawing trifluoromethyl groups.

Several approaches can be used to synthesize the metal trifluoroacetylacetonates and in many instances these may be preferable to methods employing ammonium trifluoroacetylacetonate. For metals that readily form ammine complexes, it is best to avoid using the ammonium salt. Buffering or neutralization can be effectively accomplished with sodium acetate, sodium carbonate, or with sodium or potassium hydroxide[73].

In syntheses in non-aqueous solvents, buffering or neutralization is often unnecessary. Zirconium and hafnium trifluoroacetylacetonates can be prepared in carbon tetrachloride by the action of trifluoroacetylacetone on a suspension of the anhydrous metal chlorides[16,74]. There are other advantages in utilizing non-aqueous solvents for syntheses. The by-products are often gaseous, simplifying the purification procedure. In the above reaction, for example, gaseous hydrogen chloride evolves from the solution as the chelate is formed. More important, competition for the coordination sites by the nucleophilic solvent, water, is avoided. Non-aqueous preparative routes are even more important for the hexafluoroacetylacetonates, owing to the unusual behavior of this ligand towards water.

Hexafluoroacetylacetone can be synthesized by condensation of ethyl trifluoroacetate and trifluoroacetone by sodium ethoxide[33]. It is a colorless liquid, density 1.46 g ml^{-1} with reported[33,49] boiling points ranging from 63 to 70°C. It forms an ammonium salt in much the same ways as described earlier for trifluoroacetylacetone, but the salt is much more stable in crystalline form than the trifluoroacetylacetonate[70,75]. Hexafluoroacetylacetone readily reacts with water to form a tetrahydroxy compound[48]:

$$\underset{\overset{\displaystyle |\colon \qquad \colon|}{O\cdots H\cdots O}}{CF_3-C\text{---}CH\text{---}C-CF_3} + 2H_2O \rightarrow CF_3-\underset{\underset{\displaystyle OH}{|}}{\overset{\overset{\displaystyle OH}{|}}{C}}-CH_2-\underset{\underset{\displaystyle OH}{|}}{\overset{\overset{\displaystyle OH}{|}}{C}}-CF_3$$

Infrared evidence supports the postulated structure of the product[49]; there is an intense O—H stretching vibration at 3330 cm^{-1} and the carbonyl stretch region is devoid of absorption peaks. The tetrahydroxy compound is a white crystalline solid, soluble in water and ether and slightly soluble in benzene and petroleum ether. It is very volatile and sublimes at an appreciable rate even at room temperature. It can be dehydrated by treatment with 98 per cent sulfuric acid[49].

Unquestionably, the tetrahydroxy compound is a poorer coordinating moiety than the anhydrous enol, and this may be the reason that several attempts to synthesize metal hexafluoroacetylacetonates in aqueous solution have been unsuccessful[34]. This is not to say that the syntheses cannot be carried out in water, but only to indicate that the use of non-aqueous solvent media may be preferable in the event that difficulties are encountered in aqueous preparations. Aqueous media syntheses of the complexes of copper(II)[33], iron(II)[42], rhodium(III)[37], cobalt(II)[76] and several of the lanthanides[36,45] have been accomplished. Several non-aqueous solvents have also been used in the syntheses of the hexafluoroacetylacetonates. The complex of aluminum(III) is readily formed by the reaction of the anhydrous chloride with the ligand in carbon tetrachloride[46]. The iron(III) complex forms upon direct addition of an excess of hexafluoroacetylacetone to anhydrous ferric chloride, while treatment of zinc or manganous carbonate suspended in carbon tetrachloride yields the respective complexes[42]. Ethanol and methanol serve as excellent solvents in the syntheses of chromium(III) β-diketonates. In the preparation of chromium(III) hexafluoroacetylacetonate, chromium nitrate nonahydrate is dissolved in ethanol or methanol, the ligand is added, the solution is boiled for five minutes and evaporated under a stream of air, and the product is isolated by filtration[30].

Some of the studies on the fluorocarbon β-diketonates conducted during World War II[33-36,77] were stimulated by the urgent need to find stable volatile compounds of uranium for isotope separation. Uranium(IV) trifluoroacetylacetonate was prepared by reduction of aqueous uranyl solutions with sodium dithionate, addition of the ligand, and neutralization with sodium hydroxide[34,36]. The khaki-green crystals of the complex sublime at 100–110°C/10⁻⁴ mm without decomposition and without leaving any residue; the analogous hexafluoroacetylacetonate sublimes at 40–50°C/0.001 mm[34]. The uranyl complex of trifluoroacetylacetone, $UO_2(tfa)_2$, decomposes to give trifluoroacetylacetone when heated at 160°C/ 10⁻⁴ mm. Schlesinger et al.[77] have measured the vapor tensions of the uranyl and uranium(IV) complexes of trifluoroacetylacetone at 130°C and have reported the values, 0.0027 and 0.08 mm, respectively.

Metal carbonyls can be converted to trifluoro- or hexafluoro-acetylacetonates by reactions that are facilitated by ultraviolet irradiation[78,79]. Iron(III) and chromium(III) hexafluoroacetyl-acetonates have been formed via this route. By-product hydrogen and carbon monoxide are produced in stoichiometric amounts. Dunne and Cotton[79] have prepared molybdenum(III) and chromium(III) trifluoroacetylacetonates by refluxing the hexa-carbonyls in trifluoroacetylacetone. The reaction of dicobalt octacarbonyl with hexafluoroacetylacetone yields cobalt(II) hexafluoroacetylacetonate dihydrate as the principal product and a small amount of cobalt(III) hexafluoroacetylacetonate[80]. The latter sublimes readily at 45°C/0.01 mm pressure. The action of hexafluoroacetylacetone on $Mn(CO)_5Cl$ in acetonitrile produces $Mn(CO)_4(hfa)$, a rare example of a mixed carbonyl-β-diketonate-complex[80]. The product, a bright yellow solid, is diamagnetic, a non-electrolyte in nitromethane, and readily sublimes (45°C/0.01 mm).

The higher fluoroalkyl homologs of hexafluoroacetylacetone have been synthesized by condensation of trifluoroacetone with the appropriate perfluoroalkyl ethyl ester in the presence of sodium methoxide[50]. As an example, 1,1,1,5,5,6,6,7,7,7-decafluoro-2,4-heptanedione, H(dfhd), was prepared by the dropwise addition of trifluoroacetone to a mixture of ethyl heptafluorobutyrate and sodium methoxide. After standing overnight, the reaction mixture was purified by washing the ether solution with portions of dilute acid and water, dried and further purified by shaking with anhydrous sodium sulfate and then concentrated sulfuric acid. The diketone was isolated by two successive fractional distillations (b. p. 99–105°C) in 72 per cent yield. 1,1,1,5,5,6,6,6-Octafluoro-2,4-hexanedione, H(ofhd), was synthesized in a similar manner[50].

Only a few of the complexes of the higher fluoroalkyl homologs have been studied in any detail; so it is premature to attempt to draw general conclusions about their physical or chemical properties. Cr(ofhd)$_3$ and Cr(dfhd)$_3$ can be synthesized by the method reported by Sievers, Morris and Moshier[30] for the preparation of Cr(hfa)$_3$. Both complexes are dark-green mobile liquids at room temperature. The zirconium and hafnium complexes of H(dfhd) were prepared by the reaction of the anhydrous metal chlorides with the ligands in anhydrous benzene[50]. The complexes were purified by fractional distillation in a molecular still at 70°C/0.001–0.01 mm. From the limited number of examples available, e.g. Cr(ofhd)$_3$, Cr(dfhd)$_3$, Zr(dfhd)$_4$ and Hf(dfhd)$_4$, it would seem that the complexes are roughly comparable in volatility to the hexafluoroacetylacetonates.

Properties of the Metal Complexes

Probably the most thoroughly studied complexes are those of copper(II). Gillard and Wilkinson[81] have shown by ebullioscopic measurements that copper(II) trifluoroacetylacetonate is monomeric in benzene and chlorobenzene. It is square planar but forms weak adducts with ethanol and acetone and much more stable adducts with pyridine by coordination in the fifth and sixth positions[49,81]. It exhibits thermochromism in toluene, xylene, chloroform, chlorobenzene and benzene, the color of the solutions changing from royal-blue when cold to green when boiling. The thermochromism has been attributed to thermal broadening of the first allowed electronic transition[81].

Dipole moment measurements suggest that copper(II) and cobalt(II) trifluoroacetylacetonates in benzene are square planar with *cis-trans* ratios of about 3:2[82,83], but the configurations and isomer distributions have not been definitely established. Infrared, ultraviolet and visible spectral studies have been made on the copper(II) complexes of trifluoroacetylacetone and hexa-fluoroacetylacetone[34,49,84–86]. The most dominant effect observed in these studies is the electron-withdrawing tendency of the trifluoromethyl groups. This factor is probably responsible for the lower solvolytic stability in dioxane–water solutions of the tri-fluoro- and hexafluoro- complexes compared to the analogous acetylacetonates[72,87].

The nuclear magnetic resonance spectra of the fluorocarbon β-diketonate chelates show shifts which are probably attributable to the inductive effect. There is a down-field shift in the resonance peaks arising from the methylene protons as the number of trifluoromethyl groups is increased. This is graphically demonstrated in the spectra of the mixed-ligand complexes obtained by ligand exchange reactions of aluminum acetylacetonate with aluminum hexafluoroacetylacetonate[88]. The methylene resonance peak of aluminum acetylacetonate in carbon tetrachloride appears at 5.37 ppm (δ) relative to tetramethylsilane, while the peak is shifted down-field to 6.55 ppm for the hexafluoroacetylacetonate. As expected, the peaks for the mixed-ligand complexes appear at intermediate positions. The non-identical methylene protons in each of the two mixed-ligand complexes are progressively de-shielded in a regular fashion with the increasing electron affinity of attached groups. For $Al(hfa)(acac)_2$ the peaks occur at 5.53 and 6.20 ppm for the acac and hfa moieties, respectively; the peaks for $Al(hfa)_2(acac)$ are found at 5.68 (acac) and 6.37 ppm (hfa).

A survey study[70] of gas phase reactions of several trifluoro- and hexafluoroacetylacetonates bears directly on the problems that may arise in gas phase chromatography. It was learned that copper(II) hexafluoroacetylacetonate deposits elemental copper when a stream of nitrogen carrying the complex is passed through a glass tube heated to 275°C. In hydrogen, the trifluoro- and hexafluoro-compounds are easily reduced, forming a deposit of metallic copper at temperatures as low as 250°C. This emphasizes the necessity for taking care not to operate the injection port of the chromatography apparatus at excessively high temperatures. It also indicates that hydrogen should not be used as a carrier gas when high temperatures are to be encountered. Gas phase reactions of hydrogen with the hexafluoroacetylacetonate complexes of cobalt(II) and nickel(II) also yield metallic deposits at 250°C[70].

The remarkable stability of chromium(III) hexafluoroacetylacetonate deserves special comment. The complex is stable in a nitrogen atmosphere at temperatures up to about 375°C; and it shows no tendency to be reduced or decompose in the gas phase in hydrogen at temperatures up to about 400°C[70]. It is readily steam distilled from boiling water and distils unchanged from boiling aqua regia or concentrated sulfuric acid[30,78]. With such unusual properties, the complex is certain to evoke further interest.

The zirconium and hafnium complexes of trifluoroacetylacetone have been the subject of several studies[69,89–92] Schultz and Larsen[69] were able to separate the zirconium and hafnium complexes by multiple solvent-extraction operations. An attempt to separate the complexes by fractional sublimation was only partially successful[89]. An equimolar mixture was sublimed at 160°C/1.5–2.0 mm until about 45 per cent of the sample had collected on a cold finger. The sublimate contained 59 per cent of the total hafnium and 30 per cent of the total zirconium, indicating that the hafnium complex is slightly more volatile. Recent nuclear magnetic resonance studies have indicated that mixtures of solutions of zirconium trifluoroacetylacetonate and zirconium acetylacetonate yield mixed-ligand complexes by rapid ligand exchange reactions.[92]

Jarrett[93] has made paramagnetic resonance absorption measurements on iron(III) and chromium(III) trifluoro- and hexafluoroacetylacetonates. Resonance was observed in Cr(tfa)$_3$, Fe(tfa)$_3$, and Cr(hfa)$_3$, but could not be detected in Fe(hfa)$_3$ although magnetic susceptibility measurements showed that it is paramagnetic. The crystal structure of chromium(III) hexafluoroacetylacetonate is hexagonal, while the analogous iron(III) complex crystallizes in two forms, tetragonal and hexagonal structures.

Because trifluoroacetylacetone is unsymmetrical, valuable stereochemical information may be obtained by studying the complexes of this ligand. Fay and Piper[94,95] have demonstrated that the trifluoroacetylacetonates of trivalent metal ions may exist in *cis* and *trans* isomeric configurations. The isomers of the cobalt(III) and rhodium(III) complexes were separated by liquid–solid column chromatography on an alumina column using benzene–hexane mixtures as the eluent. In both instances the *trans* isomer was eluted first and the *cis* isomer, expected to be more polar, was eluted last. The identity of the isomers was established by their unique nuclear magnetic resonance spectra. In the *cis* isomer all three methyl groups, all three methylene protons and all three trifluoromethyl groups are equivalent by a three-fold rotation axis. Single peaks are found in the methyl and methylene regions of the proton spectra and also in the ^{19}F magnetic resonance spectra. In the *trans* isomer, which has no symmetry, the methyl, methylene and trifluoromethyl groups are all non-equivalent. Therefore one finds multiple peaks in each of the regions, affording a ready means of distinguishing the isomers. The chromium(III) complex is paramagnetic; so n.m.r. spectroscopy could not be used directly to detect *cis–trans* isomerism. However, Fay and Piper were able to separate the isomers by liquid–solid chromatography and to establish their identities by X-ray powder pattern measurements. The more readily eluted, less soluble isomer is isomorphous with the *trans* complexes of cobalt(III) and rhodium(III). In solutions at equilibrium the isomer distribution for the chromium(III), rhodium(III) and cobalt(III) complexes is approximately 80 per cent *trans* to 20 per cent *cis*.

One might wonder whether geometrical isomerism in chelates with unsymmetrical ligands will complicate the quantitative gas chromatographic determination of metals by giving rise to multiple peaks. As it happens, the isomers generally are eluted together with almost identical retention times, so no complication occurs. Conditions can sometimes be found under which the isomers of non-labile complexes are partially or totally separated[16] (see Chapter 5). Therefore when broad, split, or unsymmetrical chromatographic peaks are obtained, it should be borne in mind that the cause may lie in the isomerism of the complexes. Even the complexes that can be isolated in only one stable configuration[94], e.g. the *trans* isomers of the aluminum, gallium(III), indium(III), manganese(III) and iron(III) trifluoroacetylacetonates, may give broadened chromatographic peaks due to isomerization during elution. The extent of broadening induced by rapid isomerization of labile complexes will depend on how greatly the polarity and volatility of the isomeric forms differ. For the trifluoroacetylacetonates studied so far isomerization has not caused any serious difficulties[2].

REFERENCES

1. W. D. Ross, *Anal. Chem.*, **35**, 1596 (1963).
2. W. D. Ross and G. Wheeler, Jr., *Anal. Chem.*, **36**, 266 (1964); W. D. Ross, R. E. Sievers and G. Wheeler, Jr., *Anal. Chem.*, **37**, 598 (1965).
3. R. S. Juvet and R. Durbin, *J. Gas Chromatography*, **1**, 14 (Dec. 1963).
4. W. W. Brandt and J. E. Heveran, 142nd National Meeting, American Chemical Society, Atlantic City, New Jersey, Sept. 9–14, 1962.
5. A. I. M. Keulemans, *Gas Chromatography, 1960*, Ed. by R. P. W. Scott, Butterworths, 1960, Washington, p. 307.
6. R. W. Moshier, J. E. Schwarberg, R. E. Sievers and M. L. Morris, 14th Conference on Analytical Chemistry and Applied Spectroscopy, Pittsburgh, Pa., March 5, 1963.
7. K. Knox, S. Y. Tyree, Jr., R. D. Srivastava, V. Norman, J. Y. Bassett, Jr. and J. H. Holloway, *J. Am. Chem. Soc.*, **79**, 3358 (1957) and references cited therein.
8. A. B. Bardawil, F. N. Collier, Jr. and S. Y. Tyree, Jr., *Inorg. Chem.*, **3**, 149 (1964).
9. J. B. Evans and J. E. Willard, *J. Am. Chem. Soc.*, **78**, 2908 (1956).
10. J. Tadmor, Israel Atomic Energy Commission Preprint IA-785.
11. J. Tadmor, *J. Inorg. Nuclear. Chem.*, **23**, 158 (1961); J. Tadmor, *Anal. Chem.*, **36**, 1565 (1964).
12. M. Lederer, *Nature*, **176**, 462 (1955).
13. A. A. Duswalt, Jr., Doctoral Dissertation, Purdue University, 1958.
14. W. V. Floutz, Masters Thesis, Purdue University 1959.
15. T. Fujinaga, T. Kuwamoto and Y. Ono, *Bunseki Kagaku*, **12**, (12), 1199 (1963); *C.A.*, **60**, 6209 (1964).
16. R. E. Sievers, B. W. Ponder, M. L. Morris and R. W. Moshier, *Inorg. Chem.*, **2**, 693 (1963).
17. W. J. Biermann and H. Gesser, *Anal. Chem.*, **32**, 1525 (1960).
18. W. W. Brandt, *Gas Chromatography*, 1960, Ed. by R. P. W. Scott, Butterworths, 1960, Washington, p. 305.
19. R. G. Melcher, Masters Thesis, Purdue University, 1961.
20. J. E. Heveran, Masters Thesis, Purdue University, 1962.
21. R. D. Hill and H. Gesser, *J. Gas Chromatography*, **1**, 11, (Oct. 1963).
22. R. D. Hill, Masters Thesis, University of Manitoba, 1962.
23. J. Janak, *Gas Chromatography*, 1960, Ed. by R. P. W. Scott, Butterworths, 1960, Washington, p. 306.

24. R. E. SIEVERS, B. W. PONDER and R. W. MOSHIER, 141st National Meeting, American Chemical Society, Washington, D.C., March 24, 1962.
25. K. YAMAKAWA, K. TANIKAWA and K. ARAKAWA, *Chem. Pharm. Bull.* *(Tokyo)*, **11**, (11), 1405 (1963); *C.A.*, **60**, 7464 (1964).
26. R. G. CHARLES and M. A. PAWLIKOWSKI, *J. Phys. Chem.*, **62**, 440 (1958).
27. J. VON HOENE, R. G. CHARLES and W. M. HICKAM, *J. Phys. Chem.*, **62**, 1098 (1958).
28. W. G. BALDWIN, Masters Thesis, University of Manitoba, 1961.
29. R. E. SIEVERS, Dayton Gas Chromatography Discussion Group Meeting, Dayton, Ohio, November 1961.
30. R. E. SIEVERS, R. W. MOSHIER and M. L. MORRIS, *Inorg. Chem.*, **1**, 966 (1962).
31. R. E. SIEVERS, American Chemial Society 16th Annual Summer Symposium on Analytical Chemistry, Tucson, Arizona, June 19, 1963; *Chem. and Eng. News*, **41**, 41 (July 1, 1963).
32. J. E. SCHWARBERG, Masters Thesis, University of Dayton, 1964; J. E. SCHWARBERG, R. W. MOSHIER and J. H. WALSH, *Talanta*, **11**, 1213 (1964).
33. A. L. HENNE, M. S. NEWMAN, L. L. QUILL and R. A. STANIFORTH, *J. Am. Chem. Soc.*, **69**, 1819 (1947).
34. R. N. HASZELDINE, W. K. MUSGRAVE, F. SMITH and L. M. TURTON, *J. Chem. Soc.*, 609 (1951).
35. H. GILMAN, R. G. JONES, E. BINDSCHADLER, D. BLUME, G. KARMAS, G. A. MARTIN, JR., J. B. NOBIS, J. R. THIRTLE, H. L. YALE and F. A. YOEMAN, *J. Am. Chem. Soc.*, **78**, 2790 (1956).
36. R. A. STANIFORTH, Doctoral Dissertation, Ohio State University, 1943.
37. J. P. COLLMAN, R. L. MARSHALL, W. L. YOUNG and S. D. GOLDBY *Inorg. Chem.*, **1**, 704 (1962).
38. R. E. SIEVERS and R. G. LINCK, unpublished data.
39. W. G. SCRIBNER, J. D. WEIS and R. W. MOSHIER, 148th National Meeting American Chemical Society, Chicago, Ill., Sept. 1964.
40. D. K. ALBERT, *Anal. Chem.*, **36**, 2034 (1964).
41. W. D. ROSS, private communication to R. E. Sievers, October 1963.
42. M. L. MORRIS, R. W. MOSHIER and R. E. SIEVERS, *Inorg. Chem.*, **2**, 411 (1963).
43. J. C. BAILAR, JR. and D. H. BUSCH, *Chemistry of the Coordination Compounds*, Reinhold, New York, 1956, p. 42 and references cited therein.
44. E. O. BRIMM, Doctoral Dissertation, University of Illinois, 1940.
45. N. J. ROSE, private communication to R. E. Sievers, June 1, 1964.
46. M. L. MORRIS, R. W. MOSHIER and R. E. SIEVERS, *Inorg. Syn.*, **8**, in press.
47. H. FREISER, *Anal. Chem.*, **31**, 1440 (1959).
48. B. G. SCHULTZ and E. M. LARSEN, *J. Am. Chem. Soc.*, **71**, 3250 (1949).
49. R. L. BELFORD, A. E. MARTELL and M. CALVIN, *J. Inorg. Nuclear Chem.*, **2**, 11 (1956).
50. B. H. SMITH, R. W. MOSHIER and R. E. SIEVERS, unpublished data.
51. G. S. HAMMOND, D. C. NONHEBEL and C. S. WU, *Inorg. Chem.*, **2**, 73 (1963).
52. F. A. COTTON and J. S. WOOD, *Inorg. Chem.*, **3**, 245 (1964) and references cited therein.
53. R. G. CHARLES and A. LANGER, *J. Phys. Chem.*, **63**, 603 (1959).
54. E. KLESPER, A. H. CORWIN and D. A. TURNER, *J. Org. Chem.*, **27**, 700 (1962).

55. R. S. JUVET, JR. and F. M. WACHI, *Anal. Chem.*, **32**, 290 (1960); F. M. WACHI, Doctoral Dissertation, University of Illinois, 1959.
56. R. A. KELLER, *J. Chromatog.*, **5.**, 225 (1961).
57. H. W. MYERS and R. F. PUTNAM, *Anal. Chem.*, **34**, 664 (1962).
58. F. ZADO, *New Nuclear Materials Including Non-Metallic Fuels*, Vol. II., International Atomic Energy Agency, Vienna, 1963, p. 49.
59. R. A. KELLER and H. FREISER, *Gas Chromatography*, 1960, Ed. by R. P. W. SCOTT, Butterworths, London, 1960, p. 301.
60. J. TADMOR, *Research Council of Israel, Bulletin, Chem. Soc.*, **10A**, No. 3: 17 (Sept. 1961); *Ibid*, **11A**, No. 2: 144 (July 1962); J. TADMOR, *J. Gas Chromatography*, **2**, 385 (1964).
61. L. G. VLASOV, Y. N. SYCHEV and A. V. LAPITSKII, *Vestn. Mosk. Univ.*, Ser. II, *Khim*, **17**, (6), 55 (1962); *C.A.*, **60**, 2530 (1964).
62. A. G. HAMLIN, G. IVESON and T. R. PHILLIPS, *Anal. Chem.*, **35**, 2037 (1963), and references cited therein.
63. J. F. ELLIS, C. W. FORREST and P. L. ALLEN, *Anal. Chim. Acta*, **22**, 27 (1960).
64. J. F. ELLIS and C. W. FORREST, *J. Inorg. Nuclear Chem.*, **16**, 150 (1960).
65. J. H. BOCHINSKI, K. W. GARDINER and R. S. JUVET, JR., *Ultrapurification of Semi-Conductors*, Ed. by M. S. BROOKS and J. W. KENNEDY, Macmillan New York, 1962, p. 239; J. I. PETERSON, L. M. KINDLEY and H. E. PODALL, *ibid.*, p. 253.
66. R. S. JUVET, JR. and T. TIVEN, Pittsburgh Conference on Analytical Chemistry and Applied Spectroscopy, March 4–8, 1963.
67. G. T. MORGAN and H. W. MOSS, *J. Chem. Soc.*, **105**, 189 (1914), *et seq.*, and references cited therein.
68. J. C. REID and M. CALVIN, *J. Am. Chem. Soc.*, **72**, 2948 (1950).
69. B. G. SCHULTZ and E. M. LARSEN, *J. Am. Chem. Soc.*, **72**, 3610 (1950).
70. L. B. SPENDLOVE, Masters Thesis, Air Force Institute of Technology, 1963
71. R. C. YOUNG, *Inorg. Syn.* **2**, 25 (1946).
72. L. G. VAN UITERT, W. C. FERNELIUS and B. E. DOUGLAS, *J. Am. Chem. Soc.*, **75**, 457 (1953).
73. E. W. BERG and J. T. TRUEMPER, *J. Phys. Chem.*, **64**, 487 (1960) and references cited therein.
74. M. L. MORRIS, R. W. MOSHIER and R. E. SIEVERS, *Inorg. Syn.*, **9**, in press.
75. A. G. CUPKA, JR., Masters Thesis, Air Force Institute of Technology, 1963.
76. F. A. COTTON and R. H. HOLM, *J. Am. Chem. Soc.*, **82**, 2979 (1960).
77. H. I. SCHLESINGER, H. C. BROWN, J. J. KATZ, S. ARCHER and R. A. LAD, *J. Am. Chem. Soc.*, **75**, 2446 (1953).
78. J. C. GOAN, C. H. HUETHER and H. PODALL, *Inorg. Chem.*, **2**, 1078 (1963).
79. T. G. DUNNE and F. A. COTTON, *Inorg. Chem.*, **2**, 263 (1963).
80. M. KILNER and A. WOJCICKI, 148th National Meeting, American Chemical Society, Chicago, Ill., Sept. 1964.
81. R. D. GILLARD and G. WILKINSON, *J. Chem. Soc.*, 5885 (1963).
82. R. H. HOLM and F. A. COTTON, *J. Inorg. Nuclear Chem.*, **15**, 63 (1960).
83. P. J. McCARTHY and A. E. MARTELL, *J. Am. Chem. Soc.*, **78**, 2106 (1951).
84. H. F. HOLTZCLAW, JR. and J. P. COLLMAN, *J. Am. Chem. Soc.*, **79**, 3318 (1957).

85. K. NAKAMOTO, Y. MORIMOTO and A. E. MARTELL, *J. Phys. Chem.*, **66**, 346 (1962).
86. J. P. FACKLER, JR., F. A. COTTON and D. W. BARNUM, *Inorg. Chem.*, **2**, 97 (1963).
87. H. F. HOLTZCLAW, JR., A. H. CARLSON and J. P. COLLMAN, *J. Am. Chem. Soc.*, **78**, 1838 (1956).
88. R. G. LINCK and R. E. SIEVERS, 148th National Meeting, American Chemical Society, Chicago, Ill., Sept. 1964.
89. M. A. JOHNSON, Masters Thesis, University of Colorado, 1949.
90. E. M. LARSEN, G. TERRY and J. LEDDY, *J. Am. Chem. Soc.*, **75**, 5107 (1953).
91. E. M. LARSEN and G. TERRY, *J. Am. Chem. Soc.*, **75**, 1560 (1953).
92. A. C. ADAMS and E. M. LARSEN, *J. Am. Chem. Soc.*, **85**, 3508 (1963)
    A. C. ADAMS and E. M. LARSEN, 148th National Meeting, American Chemical Society, Chicago, Ill., Sept. 1964.
93. H. S. JARRETT, *J. Chem. Phys.*, **27**, 1298 (1957).
94. R. C. FAY and T. S. PIPER, *J. Am. Chem. Soc.*, **85**, 500 (1963).
95. R. C. FAY and T. S. PIPER, *Inorg. Chem.*, **3**, 348 (1964).

CHAPTER 3

INSTRUMENTATION
AND TECHNIQUES

SEVERAL excellent volumes have been written on the myriad aspects of gas chromatographic instrumentation and techniques. Some of these are cited at the end of the chapter[1–8], and in them the reader will find references to still other more specific or elaborate discussions. It is not within the scope of the present volume to reproduce or even to summarize the many works written on the general subject. Instead the topics will be treated from the rather restricted view of the chemist interested in using gas chromatography for metal analysis or for studies in metal coordination chemistry.

In its simplest form a gas–liquid chromatography apparatus consists of nothing more than a tube containing a liquid partitioning agent, and a detector at the end of the tube. The function of the column is to separate the mixture of compounds, while the detector measures the amount of each component. All other parts of the apparatus serve in one way or another to complement the function of the two basic units. For this reason gas chromatographic equipment is simple to operate and maintain and is quite inexpensive compared with most other forms of instrumentation.

Over one-hundred companies now market gas chromatography equipment. The equipment varies widely in price, depending mainly on the type and quality of detector and recorder, and the versatility and quality of the temperature controls, sample inlet system, and flow controls. Some workers prefer to build their own apparatus but most use commercially obtained equipment often modified to suit a particular purpose. Almost all of the studies of metal chelates have been performed on instruments of commercial origin on which only minor modifications had been made. In no

59

instance was it necessary to change the basic apparatus in any way that would reduce the effectiveness of its application to other analyses. The modifications usually consisted of substituting glass or Teflon in the flow system wherever possible so as to reduce or eliminate contact of the complexes with hot metallic surfaces. Often this involved merely using glass or Teflon columns in place of conventional ones made of stainless steel or copper[10]. With very few exceptions the detectors were of conventional design and are available from commercial sources. In the following sections, the various experimental aspects of the chromatography of metal complexes are discussed.

DETECTORS

In the selection of equipment one of the first and most important choices to be made is of the best type of detector. This will depend largely on the concentration level which the user wishes to measure. For ordinary work in the microgram range, the best detector now in general use is probably the thermal conductivity cell. For work in the ultra-trace region ranging down to quantities of metal on the order of 10^{-12} g, more sensitive detectors such as those based on ionization phenomena are required. The detectors most widely used in studies of metal chelates are the thermal conductivity detector, the electron capture detector, and the flame ionization detector.

Thermal Conductivity Detector

The thermal conductivity cell, or katharometer, was first used in gas chromatography by Claesson[9] in 1946 and is still the most commonly used form of detection today. The heart of the detector is a metal filament or a metal oxide thermistor* that senses changes in the thermal conductivity of the carrier gas stream by the fluctuations in filament resistance induced by temperature changes. The filament is maintained at a higher temperature than the cell housing; so the heat transfer is a function of the thermal

---

* At elevated temperatures thermistors are insensitive, so metal filaments are used almost exclusively.

conductivity of the gas in the cell. Because absolute changes in thermal conductivity are very difficult to measure, differential techniques are used. Two pairs of matched filaments are arranged in a Wheatstone bridge circuit housed in a cell through which there are two gas channels, a sample channel and a reference channel. The bridge is balanced as long as the,thermal conductivity of the gas flowing through the sample side of the bridge is the same as that flowing across the reference side. When the sample stream contains a foreign gas, the rate of heat transfer is changed and the bridge becomes unbalanced. The magnitude of unbalance is a measure of the instantaneous concentration of the solute in the carrier gas. The signal is fed to a recorder, thus producing the chromatogram.

The sensitivity of the thermal conductivity detector is a function of the temperature and thermal coefficient of resistance of the filaments, the thermal gradient from the filaments to the cell wall, the thermal conductivity of the carrier gas, and the cell geometry. Most commonly the filaments are made of tungsten or platinum, although other metals may also be used. Helium and hydrogen are the best carrier gases because their thermal conductivities are much higher than any of the other gases. Consequently, smaller amounts of foreign gases can be detected in the carrier gas stream than would otherwise be possible. Helium is used in preference to hydrogen because of safety considerations and the possibility that hydrogen would react with the sample.

The thermal conductivity cell is robust and easy to operate; furthermore it is non-destructive. This is an important attribute in survey studies where it is neceessary to collect samples from the eluate and examine them to determine whether or not decomposition has occurred. Thermal conductivity detectors have performed very well in several studies on metal chelates[10–15]. They are moderately sensitive by gas chromatography standards; the detection range extends from quantities of metal on the order of 10^{-4} g down to about 10^{-8} g[11]. The optimum sample volume is between *ca.* 0.2 and 20 μl; so the concentration levels that can be measured are between a few parts per million at the lower limit to saturated solutions at the upper limit. An example of the detection of a mixture of 0.0059 μg of beryllium and 11.2 μg of aluminum was shown in Fig. 2.7 (p. 30). The feasibility of using thermal conductivity detectors for the quantitative determination of mixtures of beryllium, aluminum, gallium and indium trifluoroacetylacetonates has been demonstrated[13]. The detector was shown to be capable of detecting quantities of metal between 0.2 and 60 μg with overall relative mean errors of 2 per cent based on calibration curves using peak areas and 2.4 per cent using peak heights. From the standpoint of convenience the thermal conductivity cell is probably the most satisfactory detection device for survey studies and for quantitative determinations in which only moderate sensitivity is required.

Several investigators have used thermal conductivity detectors in studies on metal halides[16–21]. The reactivity of the metal halides poses problems in the use of these detectors that are not encountered to any noticeable extent with the metal chelates. In some instances it was considered necessary to construct special cells of corrosion-resistant materials[19,21]. In the metal halide studies the katharometer filaments were made of either nickel[19,21] or platinum[16,17,20].

Electron Capture Ionization Detector

In the absence of externally imposed effects gases are excellent electrical insulators, but if they are caused to ionize, they will conduct an electrical current. The measurement of differences in the current is the common underlying basis for all ionization detectors. The manner in which ionization is induced may take several forms: e.g. radioactive sources, usually α- or β-rays; flame ionization, in which the gases are burned in a flame; and thermionic emission, in which electrons are emitted from a heated cathode. The ease of ionization of various gases differs greatly and this is the reason for the selectivity and, indirectly, the remarkable sensitivity of the ionization detectors. The principles of operation of the various ionization detectors have been reviewed by Lovelock[22]. Most detectors measure the increase in current, above that due to the background ionization of the carrier gas, resulting when a more readily ionized gas appears in the carrier stream. The electron capture detector is an exception; it measures a decrease rather than an increase in current.

To understand how the electron capture detector operates, one must consider the nature of recombination phenomena. The principal process causing the loss of ions at low field strengths is the recombination of negative and positive ions. The recombination between a positive ion and a free electron is on the order of 10^5 to 10^8 less likely than between oppositely charged molecular ions. The extent of recombination at low field strength will depend on the identity of the negative charge carriers. In argon or nitrogen these are free electrons, so recombination is less likely than in gases with large electron affinities where free electrons are rapidly captured to form negative molecular ions.

Lovelock and Lipsky[22,23] designed the electron capture detector to exploit recombination phenomena. A β-ray source such as a foil containing tritium or some other radioactive nuclide is used in the detector to generate electrons. The ion chamber containing a free electron gas such as nitrogen is kept at a potential just sufficient to collect all of the free electrons formed. When an electron-capturing gas is introduced, a corresponding reduction in current flow results. Because the electron affinity of various compounds differs so greatly, the detector is extremely sensitive to some compounds while insensitive to others. Halogenated compounds can be detected in nanogram and picogram quantities while hydrocarbons produce little or no response.

The high sensitivity of the electron capture detector to fluorocarbon β-diketonate complexes makes the device extremely valuable in detecting ultra-trace quantities of metals[24,25]. The early studies showed that quantities of chromium as small as 2×10^{-12} g can be detected. The limit of detectability was imposed by the presence of trace impurities in the solvent, toluene, rather than by noise or the inability of the detector to respond to lower concentrations of the complex. More recent studies have pushed the limit of detectability of chromium to even smaller amounts[25,26]. The electron affinity of the chelates is a function both of the metal ion and the extent of halogenation in the ligand. The detector is much more sensitive to the trifluoro- and hexafluoro-acetylacetonates than to the analogous acetylacetonates. Under comparable but not necessarily optimum conditions the limit of detectability of chromium(III) acetylacetonate is 2.5×10^{-10} mole while the limit for the trifluoroacetylacetonate is 1.8×10^{-13} mole and for the hexafluoro-compound is 4.9×10^{-14} mole[24]. The trend reflects the increasing extent of substitution of the highly electronegative trifluoromethyl groups. A similar trend was found in the detection limits of the aluminum complexes with the same three ligands. The response of the detector is also strongly dependent on the metal ion; a given concentration of chromium(III) trifluoroacetyl-acetonate produces about ten times the signal that the aluminum complex gives. Furthermore, by varying the applied potential, one can enhance or depress the signal arising from each of the complexes. This affords a measure of selectivity in detection sur-passed only by the flame photometric detector among the devices so far studied.

Perhaps the most impressive demonstrations of the performance of the electron capture detector are to be found in the quantitative studies on chromium(III) hexafluoroacetylacetonate and the aluminum(III), rhodium(III) and chromium(III) trifluoroacetyl-acetonates[25,26]. The calibration curve for chromium(III) hexafluoroacetylacetonate covers a total concentration range from 100 to 0.004 ppm Cr. The results obtained for rhodium(III) trifluoroacetylacetonate are equally impressive, the limit of detectability being about 2×10^{-12} gram of rhodium[25]. Thus, the great sensitivity of the electron capture detector has made it possible to detect smaller traces of some metals than has previously been achieved by other analytical methods.

Figure 3.1 shows the chromatograms for five successive analyses of solutions of Cr(hfa)$_3$ dissolved in toluene[27]. To obtain such reproducible chromatograms one must exercise careful control over manipulative and environmental variables. The use of chloroform in the solutions as an internal standard, with subsequent normaliza-tion of the signal, serves to decrease the errors due to variations in sample size and to small fluctuations in the sensitivity of detector response. In Fig. 3.2 chromatograms are shown for replicate samples of 5.2×10^{-8} g ml^{-1} of Cr(hfa)$_3$ in toluene. The reproduci-bility is exceptionally good considering that the analyses are being performed at the parts per billion level. The calibration curves are not linear over wide concentration ranges but they are regular and do not deviate so seriously as to be troublesome[25] (see Chapter 4).

The instrument used for most of the electron capture studies was equipped with a ^{90}Sr radiation source housed in a detector cell originally designed as a diode ionization detector[24,25]. By very simple modifications the detector was converted to operate on the electron capture principle. Tritium sources (as titanium tritide) have also been used[26], but the data are insufficient to allow a comparison of the merits of the two sources.

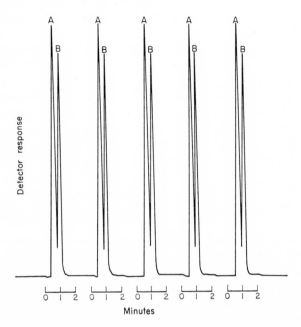

FIG. 3.1. Chromatograms of successive analyses of Cr(hfa)$_3$, 1.3×10^{-3} g ml^{-1} concentration[27]. A: Cr(hfa)$_3$; B: CHCl$_3$ (internal standard). *Column:* 11 ft $\times \frac{1}{8}$ in. o.d., stainless steel, packed with 20 per cent D.C. Silicone 71OR on Gas Chrom Z. *Instrument:* Barber Colman Model 20, electron capture detector. *Solvent:* toluene. *Sample size:* 2 μl. *Column temp.:* 90°C. *Nitrogen flow rate:* 67 ml min^{-1}. *Detector voltage:* 17 V.

The performance of the electron capture detector is strongly affected by the type of solvent in which the chelates are dissolved[24,25]. Solvents with high electron affinities, e.g. carbon tetrachloride and other halogenated compounds, must be avoided if the detector is to respond faithfully. Benzene and toluene have been employed with excellent results.

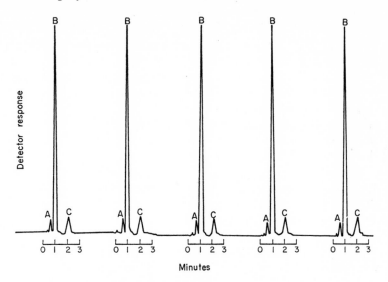

FIG. 3.2. Chromatograms of successive analyses of Cr(hfa)₃, 5.2×10^{-8} g ml⁻¹ concentration[27]. A: Cr(hfa)₃; B: CHCl₃ (internal standard); C: impurity in toulene. Same column, instrument and column conditions as in Fig. 3.1. *Detector voltage:* 12 V.

Flame Ionization Detector

The flame ionization detector is intermediate in sensitivity between the electron capture detector and the thermal conductivity detector. Detectors based on ionization in a hydrogen flame were designed by McWilliam and Dewar[28,29] and Harley, Nel, and Pretorius[30]. The combustion of mixtures of hydrogen and oxygen or air produces very few ions, but when carbon-containing compounds are present, ionization occurs and the flame becomes conductive. The mechanism by which ions are produced is not well understood, but whatever the mechanism, the increase in conductivity is sufficient to make the detector an effective device for measuring carbon-containing compounds.

The design of the flame ionization detector is quite simple. The effluent from the column is mixed with hydrogen and air as it passes through a jet and burns in a small flame. Two electrodes measure the electrical conductivity of the flame. In common practice the burner jet comprises one of the electrodes and the other is a wire or grid extending into the tip of the flame. The potential applied across the electrodes is sufficient to produce saturation, so an increase in voltage does not increase the current. The background current is very low, *ca.* 10^{-11} to 10^{-12} amp[22], so the presence of ion-producing compounds is readily detectable even though the efficiency of ionization is poor. The detector is insensitive to the permanent gases and to water vapor but responds very well to most organic compounds.

Because the sample is destroyed in flame ionization detection, the detector cannot be used in survey studies where examination of the eluate is necessary unless special techniques are employed. For survey studies two options are open. One may interpose a stream-splitting device between the column and the detector so that the bulk of the sample by-passes the detector and is trapped in a fraction collector. Alternatively, one may obtain a chromatogram under a given set of conditions, then extinguish the flame and repeat the experiment under the same conditions using the earlier-obtained chromatogram as a guide for collecting the fractions. In normal operation the detector requires periodic cleaning to remove deposits of metal oxides that accumulate in the combustion chamber.

The flame ionization detector has been used for quantitative studies on metal chelates of acetylacetone, trifluoroacetylacetone, and hexafluoroacetylacetone[26,31–34]. Brandt and Heveran[31] used the detector in the determination of chromium as Cr(acac)$_3$. Starting with aqueous chromium solutions, they formed the complex, extracted with carbon disulfide, and injected the solution into the chromatography apparatus. They found that the peak area was linearly related to the concentration from 0.5 to 1000 ppm of chromium in the aqueous solution. Hill and Gesser[33] reported that the introduction of fluorine atoms into the chelates decreases the response from the flame detector, which is opposite to the results obtained with the electron capture detector[24]. The uncomplexed ligands produce detector responses that stand in the ratio 1.6 : 1.0 : 1.0 for acetylacetone, trifluoroacetylacetone and hexafluoroacetylacetone, respectively[33]. Not unexpectedly, the metal ion also affects the response; the ratio of responses to the complexes does not coincide with that obtained for the uncomplexed ligands.

Argon Ionization Detector

The argon ionization detector, first described by Lovelock[35], utilizes a β-ray source to excite the argon carrier gas molecules to a non-ionized metastable state. Ionization of the vapor molecules occurs by transfer of the energy stored in the metastable atoms. Any molecule with an ionization potential less than the stored energy of the metastable argon (11.7 eV) may be ionized. An increase in current across a pair of electrodes in the detector chamber is observed when ionization occurs. Experience in detecting metal complexes with this detector is limited[36,37]; therefore the performance cannot be compared with that of other detectors.

Thermionic Emission Ionization Detector

The source of ionizing radiation in the thermionic emission detector is a heated filament. The detector takes advantage of the fact that the ionization potential of helium (24.5 eV) is much higher than that of most other gases. Ryce and Bryce[38] constructed a detector from an ionization gauge modified so that a small fraction of the column effluent enters the chamber through a leak. A potential difference is maintained between a filament and grid at 18 V, a potential not sufficient to ionize the helium. When gases of lower ionization potential enter the detector, ions are formed and the resulting current is amplified and recorded.

The thermionic emission detector has been used in studies of metal complexes[10,39] but its performance does not compare favorably with that of other types of detectors. One disadvantage is that the filament is easily poisoned; consequently the detector is rendered insensitive and the signal becomes erratic.

Flame Photometric Detector

Grant[40] described the use of flame emissivity for detecting organic compounds, and Monkman and Dubois[41] used a flame photometric detector for determining chlorinated hydrocarbons. Juvet and Durbin extended its application to the detection of metal chelates[42]. In this form of detection the column effluent is burned and the emissivity of the flame is measured with a photocell and associated optical system. The most interesting feature of the detector is its selectivity, which is derived from the unique flame emission spectra of various compounds. By changing the wavelength which the photocell detects, the operator can often screen out interferences. This can be very important when the complexes are not well-separated or when one wishes to detect trace quantities of one component in the presence of large amounts of another.

Flame photometric detectors may take several forms depending on resolution and sensitivity requirements. Juvet and Durbin[42] used a Beckman DU spectrophotometer equipped with a flame attachment. The column outlet was joined directly to the capillary of a Beckman Model 4030 atomizer-burner assembly. To illustrate the selectivity of the detector, three successive chromatograms of a mixture of chromium(III), iron(III) and rhodium(III) hexafluoro-acetylacetonates were obtained (Fig. 3.3). For the first chromatogram the detector was operated at 424.4 mμ. At this wavelength the detector responded well to the chromium complex while hardly giving any response for the iron and rhodium complexes. Two other chromatographic runs were made under the same column conditions, one with the detector set at 372.0 mμ and the other at 369.2 mμ. At the latter wavelength the rhodium complex produced a very strong signal while the chromium and iron complexes were not detectable. If the compounds are well separated and selectivity is consequently not required, the wavelength may be changed after the elution of each compound so that peaks are obtained for all of the compounds in a single chromatographic run.

Figure 3.4 shows that the detector is capable of giving an unaltered quantitative response when two complexes are co-eluted. The upper-left chromatogram shows the response to 0.73 μg of chromium; the upper-right figure shows that no enhancement or depression of the signal is produced when ten times as much of the iron complex is present. The lower two chromatograms, obtained under the same conditions excepting the detector wavelength, demonstrate the non-interference of chromium in the measurement of the iron complex.

The flame photometric detector is more sensitive than the thermal conductivity detector[42] and has approximately the same

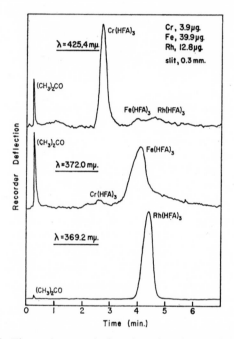

Fig. 3.3. Flame photometric detection of a mixture of Cr(hfa)₃, Fe(hfa)₃ and Rh(hfa)₃[42]. *Column:* 5 per cent D.C.-200 on silanized Chromosorb W. *Column temp.:* 67°C. *Nitrogen flow rate:* 60 ml min⁻¹. *Recorder sensitivity:* 12.5, 12.5 and 125 m.V full scale. *Oxygen-hydrogen pressure:* 10 and 1 psi, respectively.
(Courtesy of *Journal of Gas Chromatography*)

sensitivity as the flame ionization detector[43]. Studies of flame photometric detection are still in embryonic stages, but enough is known to indicate that this form of detection shows considerable promise.

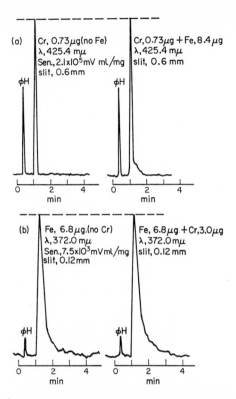

FIG. 3.4. Selectivity of flame photometric detection[42]. (A): Cr(hfa)₃ in the absence and presence of Fe(hfa)₃. (B): Fe(hfa)₃ in the absence and presence of Cr(hfa)₃. *Column:* 5 per cent D.C. High Vacuum Grease on Chromosorb W. *Column temp.:* 62°C. *Nitrogen flow rate:* 42 ml min⁻¹. *Oxygen–hydrogen pressure:* 10 and 1 psi, respectively.
(Courtesy of *Journal of Gas Chromatography*)

Other Detectors

Many other detector systems have been devised or proposed. Among these are the glow discharge, radio-frequency, gas density, radioactivity, mass spectrometer, sound velocity, and flow impedance detectors[1]. Most are untested with respect to the detection of metal compounds. Because metal complexes differ substantially from the compounds with which the detectors have been tested, the potential applicability of the detection systems cannot be assessed *a priori*.

A few of these detector systems have been used to measure volatile metal compounds. The gas density detector was used by Ellis, Forrest and Allen[44,45] for detecting corrosive gaseous mixtures of UF_6, Cl_2, Br_2, HF, ClF and BrF_5. In work with highly reactive materials this detector has the distinct advantage that the sensing elements do not come in contact with the corrosive constituents. Tadmor[46,47] has utilized radioactivity detectors in his studies of metal halides. This requires, of course, that either the halogen or the metal be labeled with a radioactive isotope. Usually the compounds were labeled with β-emitting isotopes such as ^{36}Cl, but in some of the experiments they were labeled with γ-emitting nuclides. Keulemans has given a brief report of some studies of metal halides in which the column effluent is fed into a flame, and atomic absorption is employed[48].

COLUMNS

The two principal types of columns for gas–liquid chromatography are packed columns and capillary columns. In packed columns the liquid partitioning phase is supported on a powdered solid which is contained by the tube. In capillary columns the liquid phase is supported by the inner wall of a capillary tube. In studies of metal complexes, packed columns have been used almost exclusively.

Materials of Construction

The column must be constructed of a material that is inert to the compounds being chromatographed. Most commercial instruments are furnished with columns made of stainless steel or copper. For the more stable complexes, e.g. those of chromium(III), columns composed of steel or copper can be used without difficulty. However, these materials should be avoided when work with the metal halides or with any but the most stable metal complexes is contemplated[10,11]. When stainless steel columns were used in early experiments, occasionally the chromatographic peaks were distorted and the samples collected from the exit of the column were discolored[10]. The column walls apparently either reacted with some of the chelates or catalyzed their decomposition, because the difficulties were not encountered under similar conditions using glass columns. Moreover, if an uncomplexed ligand is present in a sample, it likewise will tend to react with stainless steel columns.*

Teflon and borosilicate glass appear to be the best column materials for most applications. Both materials have been used with excellent success in the chromatography of a large number of metal compounds. Glass columns have the disadvantage of being rather easily broken, but they can be used at higher temperatures than Teflon columns.

Ideally the entire flow system should be constructed of highly inert materials. Substitution of a column that is non-reactive is a simple matter, but it is not so easy to modify the detector cell. Fortunately the sample spends more than 99 per cent of its instrument residence time within the column. Unless the compounds are highly reactive, modification of the detector is usually unnecessary.

In the chromatography of metal fluorides and other reactive fluorine compounds, corrosion is a particularly acute problem. Although no material is completely inert, the difficulties may be minimized by using nickel columns and nickel-plating the other exposed surfaces.[21,44].

Solid Support

In theory, the only function of the solid support in gas–liquid chromatography is to support the liquid stationary phase in such a manner that the gas stream may pass through it. In actuality, the solid support often markedly affects the elution behavior (e.g. peak shape, retention time, and tailing) of the gaseous components. These gas–solid interactions often complicate the elution, resulting in peak tailing and irreversible adsorption or reaction at the solid support surface. To reduce such complications one should choose solid supports which are chemically inert and have a low surface adsorption activity.

---

* When trifluoroacetylacetone was passed through a stainless steel column at 135°C, a red compound, believed to be Fe(tfa)₃, was observed in the effluent stream[10].

6

The most popular solid supports are calcined diatomaceous earth* (examples of various modifications are Chromosorb W, Chromosorb P, Gas Chrom Z, Celite, C-22 firebrick, and Sil-O-Cel) and glass microbeads. Diatomaceous earth is very porous and can support liquid phases in amounts exceeding 20 per cent by weight without becoming too sticky to be easily packed. Glass microbeads are non-porous and can only support *ca.* 1 per cent of a liquid phase.

The adsorption activity of the surface of diatomaceous earth or glass microbeads may be reduced by various chemical modifications such as silanization, or acid or alkaline washing. In silanization the hydroxyl and oxide groups at the surface are treated with reactive silyl compounds to produce a surface covered with silyl groups. Dimethyldichlorosilane and hexamethyldisilazane are commonly used as silanizing agents.[50,51]

Powdered polytetrafluoroethylene (Teflon) and polytrifluoro-monochloroethylene (Kel-F) have been used to a lesser extent than the other supports, but they are invaluable for chromatographing metal fluorides and highly reactive fluorine compounds[21,44]. They do present the disadvantages of being non-porous and difficult to handle and pack owing to tendencies to become conglomerated. However, it has recently been reported that powdered Teflon can be handled with much less difficulty at low temperatures[52].

Liquid Phase

The success of a separation depends above all other factors on the proper choice of the liquid phase. The liquid phase must have low volatility so that it does not bleed from the column, and must be thermally stable and chemically inert to the compounds being chromatographed at the prevailing column temperature. It must also exhibit sufficient specificity toward the solutes to accomplish the desired separations. Solute–solvent interactions determine the relative vapor pressures of solutes above a given stationary phase. The interactions are a composite of Keesom (dipole–dipole), Debye

---

* Calcined diatomaceous earth consists of about 91 per cent silica, 4.6 per cent alumina, and small amounts of iron, calcium and magnesium oxides[49].

(dipole–induced dipole) and London (dispersion) forces, as well as hydrogen bonding and adduct formation. It is extremely difficult to assess the contribution of each of the factors; therefore the liquid phase often can only be selected on an empirical basis. There are some generalizations that can be used as guidelines, however.

Liquid phases having functional groups which are good coordinating agents should be avoided, as the use of these liquids would invite solvolysis of the complexes. The choice of a liquid phase is occasionally restricted by the thermal instability of some of the chelates. If the column temperature required to produce a reasonable rate of elution is close to the temperature at which a complex decomposes, there is not much latitude in the types of liquid phases that can be used. A liquid phase that does not interact strongly with the complex must be chosen.

The amount of liquid phase in the column varies greatly depending on the solid support and the compounds being chromatographed. With Chromosorb W or other diatomaceous earth supports the percentage of the liquid phase is usually between 5 and 30 per cent by weight. With glass microbeads the percentage is usually 0.5 per cent or less.* The use of "lightly-loaded" columns[53–55] permits column operation at lower temperatures than would otherwise be possible, but this is achieved with some sacrifice in the efficiency of separation and the size of the sample that can be accommodated. Hill and Gesser[33] have commented that lightly-loaded columns have not proved satisfactory in their laboratory for the quantitative analysis of metal β-diketonates. They cited peak tailing, solvent flooding, and incomplete separation of components as reasons for the unsatisfactory functioning. Other workers[13,31] have used lightly-loaded columns to give excellent quantitative results. Many of the chromatograms shown in Chapters 2 and 4 were obtained with lightly-loaded columns, and examination of these figures will reveal that the columns are quite useful in spite of their potential shortcomings. Lightly-loaded

---

* As the density of glass beads is considerably greater than that of diatomaceous earth, the differences in the amounts of liquid phase per unit volume are not as great as they might appear when only weight percentages are considered.

columns are of greatest value when one or more of the chelates being chromatographed is thermally unstable at the higher column temperature necessary with larger percentages of the liquid phase. If thermal decomposition is not anticipated, a much broader range of percentages and types of liquid phases can be employed.

In the absence of specific solvent–solute interactions, compounds will emerge from a column in the order of decreasing volatility. As long as the differences in the volatility of the compounds are sufficiently large, separations may be accomplished irrespective of the stationary phase used. It is only for compounds similar in volatility that one must find liquid phases exhibiting selectivity.

Of the several types of liquids employed in separating metal chelates, the best results have been obtained with the silicones. Polydimethylsiloxanes (e.g. Dow Corning High Vacuum Silicone Grease, General Electric SE-30 Silicone Gum Rubber and Dow Corning 200 Silicone Fluid) and polymethylphenylsiloxanes (e.g. Dow Corning 710, 710R and 500 Silicone Fluids) have been the most extensively used. Studies[10–13,24,25,33,56,57] have shown that many mixtures of trifluoro- or hexafluoroacetylacetonates can be separated with silicone liquids. (Refer to the chromatograms in Chapters 2 and 4.)

Biermann and Gesser[36] used Apiezon L (high molecular weight hydrocarbons) to separate the acetylacetonates of beryllium and aluminum (see Fig. 3.5). Duswalt[14] employed silicone oil and a propylene glycol-adipic acid polymer as stationary phases in his study of the acetylacetonates.

By using SE-30 Silicone Gum Rubber, Hill and Gesser[33] obtained good separations with well-defined symmetrical peaks for the acetylacetonates, trifluoroacetylacetonates, and hexafluoro-acetylacetonates of beryllium, aluminum, and chromium. When they attempted to separate mixtures containing the trifluoroacetyl-acetonates of iron(III) and copper(II), they were only partially successful. Figure 3.6 shows that the copper complex is eluted only slightly faster than the iron complex, and the peaks overlap extensively. The Canadian workers were not able to improve the separation by using different column lengths or operating conditions. This is an example of an instance in which one should seek a stationary phase that will selectively retard one of the overlapping complexes. Following is an account of a study which illustrates some of the problems encountered in finding a suitable stationary phase[58].

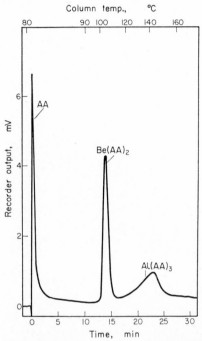

FIG. 3.5. Separation of Be(acac)₂ and Al(acac)₃ with an Apiezon L liquid stationary phase[36]. *Sample:* 0.34 μl. of a solution of the complexes in acetylacetone. *Column:* 4 ft × ¼ in., packed with 0.5 per cent Apiezon L on glass beads, 200 μ in diameter. *Column temp.:* programmed from 80 to 160°C. *Argon flow rate:* 50 ml min⁻¹.

(Courtesy of *Analytical Chemistry*)

Five stationary phases were examined: Dow Corning High Vacuum Silicone Grease, Dow Corning 710 Silicone Oil, paraffin wax, Apiezon L and polyethylene wax.* On a column containing

---

* The study was made using an F and M Scientific Corp. Model 500 instrument equipped with a thermal conductivity detector with W-2 filaments.

Dow Corning High Vacuum Silicone Grease, the extent of the separation of Cu(tfa)$_2$ and Fe(tfa)$_3$ was identical with that shown in Fig. 3.6, as was expected since the two stationary phases are chemically very similar. With Dow Corning 710 Silicone oil,

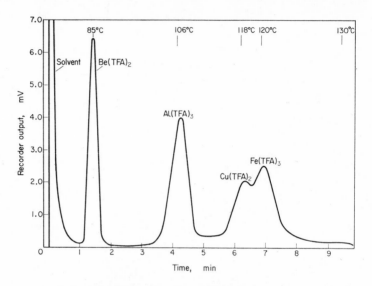

FIG. 3.6. Partial separation of Be(tfa)$_2$, Al(tfa)$_3$, Cu(tfa)$_2$ and Fe(tfa)$_3$ with a silicone gum rubber stationary phase[33]. *Column:* 1 ft × 0.06 in., i.d., packed with 7.5 per cent SE-30 on 40–60 mesh firebrick. *Column temp.:* programmed from 80 to 130°C. *Nitrogen flow rate:* 30 ml min^{-1}.
(Courtesy of *Journal of Gas Chromatography*)

resolution was improved but the separation was not complete (see Fig. 3.7). However, the order in which the complexes are eluted is reversed, the copper complex being eluted last. Specificity in solvent-solute interactions in one or both of the stationary phases is manifested unmistakably.* With Apiezon L resolution was better than with the 710 oil but broad peaks were obtained. Complete resolution was attained on a column containing paraffin wax, as seen in Fig. 3.8, but the paraffin wax bled from the column

* Other experiments were performed to demonstrate that the reversal was caused by the different liquid phases rather than by the different solid supports.

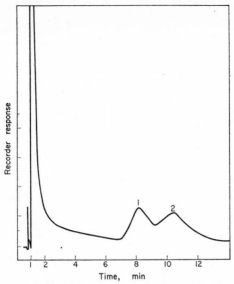

FIG. 3.7. Chromatogram of 1, Fe(tfa)$_3$ and 2, Cu(tfa)$_2$[58]. *Column:* 30 cm long × 4 mm i.d. borosilicate glass, filled with 10 per cent Dow Corning 710 Silicone oil on 60–80 mesh Chromosorb W. *Column temp.:* 100°C. *Helium flow rate:* 300 ml min^{-1}.

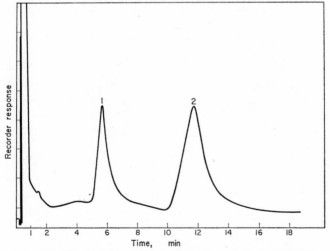

FIG. 3.8. Chromatogram of 1, Fe(tfa)$_3$ and 2, Cu(tfa)$_2$[58]. *Column:* 61 cm long × 4 mm i.d., borosilicate glass, filled with 10 per cent paraffin wax on 60–80 mesh Gas Chrom Z. *Column temp.:* 95°C. *Helium flow rate:* 87 ml min^{-1}.

at 95°C in sufficient quantity to render it unsuitable as a stationary phase. Excellent separations were attained using polyethylene wax as the stationary phase, and the liquid showed no tendency to bleed from the column at 95°C. As seen in Fig. 3.9, the peaks are

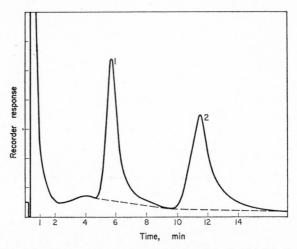

FIG. 3.9. Chromatogram of 1, Fe(tfa)$_3$ and 2, Cu(tfa)$_2$[58]. *Column:* 61 cm long × 4 mm i.d., borosilicate glass, filled with 10 per cent polyethylene wax on 60–80 mesh Gas Chrom Z. *Column temp.:* 95°C. *Helium flow rate:* 185 ml min^{-1}. The dotted line is used in measuring the adjusted peak areas for the compounds.

sharp and tailing is not appreciable. From these results it would appear that polyethylene wax will be a satisfactory stationary phase for the quantitative determination of mixtures of Fe(tfa)$_3$ and Cu(tfa)$_2$. To determine the effect of other ions, mixtures with other metal trifluoroacetylacetonates were studied using the same column. A mixture of chromium(III) and iron(III) trifluoroacetylacetonates was resolved as shown in Fig. 3.10. A mixture of aluminum, chromium(III), iron(III) and copper(II) trifluoroacetylacetonates was completely resolved (see Fig. 3.11). From this brief discussion it is easy to see how important the proper choice of the stationary phase is.

In choosing liquid phases for the chromatography of metal halides, special allowances must be made for the reactivity of the

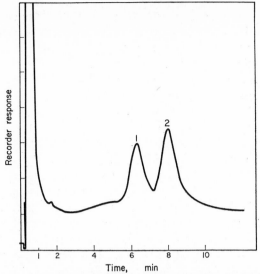

FIG. 3.10. Chromatogram of 1, Cr(tfa)$_3$ and 2, Fe(tfa)$_3$[58].
Column: 61 cm long × 4 mm i.d., borosilicate glass, filled with
10 per cent polyethylene wax on 60–80 mesh Gas Chrom Z.
Column temp.: 85°C. *Helium flow rate:* 193 ml min^{-1}.

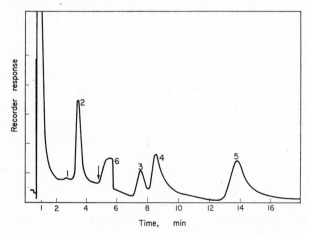

FIG. 3.11. Chromatogram of 1, unidentified; 2, Al(tfa)$_3$; 3,
Cr(tfa)$_3$; 4, Fe(tfa)$_3$; 5, Cu(tfa)$_2$; 6, elevation of base line caused
by raising the column temperature from 85 to 95°C.[58]. *Column
temp.:* initially 85°C. then raised stepwise to 95°C after 4.8 min.
Helium flow rate: 174 ml min^{-1}.

compounds. Several reports have indicated that the silicones are unsuitable because they react with the metal halides[46,47]. Freiser[59], on the other hand, reported that n-hexadecane was a suitable stationary phase for the separation of tin tetrachloride and titanium tetrachloride. Keller and Freiser[17,20] later used squalane and other hydrocarbons in their studies of tin(IV), titanium(IV), niobium(V) and tantalum(V) chlorides. In the chromatography of reactive fluorine compounds the Kel-F oils (polytrifluoromonochloroethylene) have been proven to be satisfactory partitioning liquids[21,44].

The use of molten salts as liquid partitioning agents was suggested by Juvet and Wachi[16]. One of the advantages of using fused salts is that they will withstand much higher column temperatures than any of the organic compounds commonly employed as liquid phases. If possible, the fused salt should possess a common ion with that of the solute. This serves to minimize the possibility of undesirable reactions in the column. Ion exchange in the column is one likely source of difficulty, as are redox reactions. Nitrate salts cannot be used in the separation of metal chlorides because nitrates are strong oxidizing agents and decompose in the presence of chlorides.

SAMPLE INTRODUCTION

Liquid samples and sample solutions are most simply and conveniently injected by means of a microsyringe. Metal chelates of the β-diketones are readily soluble in organic solvents, and sample solutions of definite concentration permit aliquoting by means of a calibrated syringe to obtain the desired size of sample. In the use of the microsyringe for quantitative work it is best to adopt an invariable manipulative technique. The following procedure is recommended:

1. Clean the syringe with the same solvent used for preparing the sample solution.
2. Dry the syringe by flushing with clean air.
3. Fill the syringe above the calibration mark for the size sample desired, and bring the plunger down to obtain the desired volume of sample.

4. Remove the tip of the needle from the bottle of sample, quickly wipe it, and immediately insert the needle to its full length in the injection port.
5. Empty the syringe immediately with the plunger. Use a half-second or more in emptying the syringe to obviate sample leakage back along the sides of the plunger as is more likely when exerting considerable pressure to attain instantaneous sample delivery.
6. Leave the needle in the injection port for a set period of time (illustratively, 30 sec), and then remove it.
7. Withdraw the plunger of the syringe to the position it originally occupied and read the volume of sample retained by the syringe.
8. Determine the volume of the needle by withdrawing a needle full of liquid and measuring it.
9. The volume of sample taken for injection is the sum of the reading on the barrel and the volume in the needle.
10. The volume of sample injected is the difference between volumes 9 and 7.

It is obvious that the necessity of making a number of volume measurements contributes to inaccuracy in determining the size of sample injected. For this reason there is a growing trend to use an internal standard to improve accuracy in quantitative work.

Baldwin[37] used a micropipet for sample injection. This consisted of a precision bore glass capillary tube with both ends ground to points. The tube was filled by capillary attraction of the sample solution. For injection of the sample, Baldwin disconnected the gas inlet tube, inserted the pipet and emptied it by squeezing an attached rubber bulb four times. It was then necessary to reconnect the carrier gas and start its flow in order to obtain the chromatogram. Baldwin found that about 5 per cent of the sample remained in the pipet. The maximum average deviation of peak areas was about 5 per cent and this was suggested to be the limit of reproducibility of sample injection from micropipets. This indicates that a better technique is necessary to achieve reproducible sample injection.

The injection of solid samples into the gas chromatographic port is readily accomplished by commercially available devices. In one technique a weighed sample is sealed into a thin-walled glass capillary tube* and placed in a bayonet type injector.† The device containing the sample is inserted in the instrument port, is allowed

---

* Melting point capillary tubes serve well for this purpose.
† Supplied by F & M Scientific Corp., Avondale, Pennsylvania.

to heat, and the sample tube is then broken by a plunger. The exposed sample in the hot injection port is then swept into the column by the carrier gas. This or a similar method of sample injection is required when the metal compound cannot be dissolved in a suitable solvent. The device is equally well suited for liquid samples, particularly solutions of metal halides which are easily hydrolyzed.

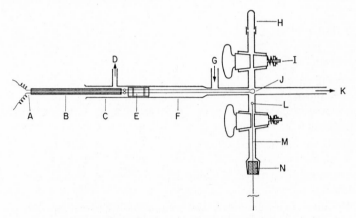

FIG. 3.12. Solid sample injection device[60].

A. Heater leads from variable 10 V power supply. B. Wooden plunger handle. C. Cylinder, 1.25 cm i.d. of Perspex, bored to contain E, and attached to the glass tube by a piece of polyethylene tubing. D. Exit for helium carrier gas, connected to a P_2O_5 drying tube. E. Cylinder of Perspex fitted with rubber O-rings made to slide readily with the outer tube and to maintain a gas-tight joint. F. Stout nichrome lead wires, 12 cm long. G. Inlet tube for helium carrier gas, connected to a P_2O_5 drying tube. H. Sample container. Fitted with stopper when weighing. I. Three-way stop cock, borosilicate glass, with outlet at end of the plug, 3- to 4-mm bore to accommodate entry of sampling spoon. J. Small crucible (wonder-stone), mounted on heating pedestal which is wound with two turns of heating wire. K. Borosilicate tube, $\frac{1}{4}$ in i.d. to injection port, connected above borosilicate tube H–K so that spoon L and handle M pass freely above crucible J. L. Nickel spoon approximately 0.3 cm long, 0.25 cm wide, 0.1 cm deep, trough-shaped. M. Nickel or stainless steel rod 0.14 cm diameter supporting spoon L. N. Rubber stopper, pressure tight, through which the rod M slides readily aided by an inert lubricant.

(Courtesy of *Analytical Chemistry*)

A solid sample injection device, described by Ellis[60], may be easily constructed. It has the advantage of permitting repetititive sampling and injection of moisture-sensitive materials such as niobium pentachloride (see Fig. 3.12). To use the device:

Attach the clean and dry device to the injection port of the gas chromatographic instrument; enclose it in a nitrogen-filled plastic bag;

sweep out the air in the device with dried carrier gas admitted at G; attach the sample holder H containing a weighed quantity of sample; obtain a sample, about 2 mg, with spoon L and empty it into the crucible J (the spoon does not empty cleanly; therefore, reweighing sample holder H gives only an approximate value of the sample); close both stopcocks; push the crucible J into the injection port using handle B; insure the immediate vaporization of the sample from the crucible by turning on the electric current to the heating pedestal.

Solvents for Sample Solution

In gas chromatography the choice of solvent for dissolution of the sample is important. It is desirable to have a highly volatile solvent for the metal chelate, a solvent which is eluted rapidly with little or no tailing of its chromatographic peak. When the solvent is eluted first, as is the usual case, and the peak tails, there is likelihood of early solute peaks being shoulders on the tail of the solvent peak. This causes difficulty in the measurement of peak areas. Brandt and Heveran[31,32] found carbon disulfide satisfactory for extracting chromium(III) acetylacetonate, and superior to other solvents in the gas chromatographic determination of the chromium chelate because the carbon disulfide did not interfere in the use of a flame ionization detector. Ross and Wheeler[25] used a solvent, toluene, which was eluted subsequent to the metal chelate in the gas chromatography of aluminum and chromium β-diketonates in the successful application of the electron capture detector. They found that benzene can be used very well for the trifluoroacetylacetonates, but it was eluted too close to the hexafluoroacetylacetonates for successful peak measurements. Impurities in solvents must be at a minimum when highly sensitive detectors such as the electron capture detector are employed because of peak interference. This detector is highly sensitive to halogenated solvents, e.g. chloroform and carbon tetrachloride; so they cannot be used. Much valuable time can be saved by evaluating an untried solvent for a given detector before attempting to use it routinely.

Solvents must be chosen which do not react with the solute or with the stationary phase of the column at the temperatures used. Likewise the solvent must not react with metal parts of the instrument or the column support material. For example, carbon tetrachloride is a highly reactive chlorinating agent and should be avoided when high temperature operation is required.

Even though a solvent may be chemically inert at the column temperature in use, highly polar solvents are tenaciously retained in the column, causing severe tailing of the solvent peak. In some instances an hour or more may be required to sweep out such solvents. Therefore, the solvent and stationary phase of the column must be so chosen that a sharp solvent peak is obtained. The flame ionization detector is insensitive to water although water is retained by the column and bleeds off rather slowly. Water is tenaciously retained by many column packings and interferes quite severely when the thermal conductivity detector is employed.

Most metal β-diketonates are soluble in benzene, carbon tetrachloride, and chloroform. For copper(II) trifluoroacetylacetonate, chloroform is preferred because of its greater solvent power for this complex. Benzene solutions of zirconium and hafnium trifluoroacetylacetonates gave well-defined peaks; however, when carbon tetrachloride was used, no chromatographic peaks other than the solvent were observed[10]. Apparently, carbon tetrachloride reacted with the complexes. Brandt[61] has observed that some of the acetylacetonate complexes also appear to react with carbon tetrachloride. Benzene or acetylacetone proved to be more satisfactory solvents. Acetone was used by Juvet and Durbin[42] as a solvent for chromium(III), iron(III) and rhodium(III) hexafluoroacetylacetonates without any difficulty. Linck and Sievers[57] have recently reported, however, that aluminum hexafluoroacetylacetonate decomposes in acetone. Several new peaks gradually appear in the nuclear magnetic resonance spectra of solutions of the complex in acetone.

Injection Port Temperature

The volatility of the metal chelates determines the column temperature for obtaining satisfactory gas chromatographic elution. The sample introduced in the injection port must arrive at the column as a narrow band in order that sharp peaks be obtained. Immediate and complete volatilization of the injected sample requires absorption of considerable thermal energy from the walls of the port. Therefore, the port temperature must be sufficiently high to obviate condensation. Otherwise, the condensed sample in the port chamber bleeds relatively slowly into the column producing broadened peaks in the resulting chromatogram. A port temperature 25–50°C higher than the column temperature has proven to be generally satisfactory, although in some cases higher port temperatures are required to insure rapid volatilization[10].

If peaks are broad, oftentimes an increase in the injection port temperature will sharpen them. Melcher[62] made this observation in studying the gas chromatographic behavior of aluminum acetylacetonate. However, he found that as he passed an injection port temperature of 290°C, a further increase in temperature resulted in the appearance of a small new peak and the size of this peak became larger at higher port temperatures with proportionate decrease in the size of the aluminum chelate peak. This was interpreted as due to thermal degradation of the metal chelate in the injection port chamber. The injection port temperature must often be a compromise. It must be high enough to cause rapid volatilization and yet not so high as to cause thermal decomposition of the complexes.

Injection Port Inserts

The authors have used readily removable borosilicate glass tubing inserts in the injection port chamber to determine the completeness of volatilization of the sample, the presence of non-volatile impurities and thermal degradation products, as well as for reducing contact of the sample with the metal of the port. After making a test run on a sample, the insert is removed and examined for deposits. If a deposit is found which is identical to the sample injected this indicates that the sample was incompletely volatilized and that a higher injection port temperature should be used. The appearance of deposits having properties different from the sample injected usually indicates thermal decomposition and suggests that a lower injection port temperature should be used. Occasionally deposits are caused by the presence of non-volatile impurities in the sample. If upon lowering the injection port temperature, no products are found in the insert and the chromatogram obtained is suitable, then the operating conditions are satisfactory.

IDENTIFICATION OF ELUATE

Identification of the eluted material under each gas chromatographic peak gives the chemist a rather complete picture of the composition of the sample and its behavior under the operating conditions used. Studies made on instruments equipped with detectors which destroy or alter the compound, for example the flame ionization detector, are not as amenable to eluate identification as when a non-destructive detector is used, unless sample splitting or special techniques are used.

Collection of the eluate under a gas chromatographic peak may be accomplished by means of a cold trap. A glass U-tube fitted with a short section of polytetrafluoroethylene (Teflon) tubing, which may be readily affixed to the exit port, is admirably suited for collection of samples from the effluent stream. Cooling the U-tube in solid carbon dioxide assures adequate trapping of the metal complex in the effluent. If gaseous, highly volatile decomposition products are to be trapped, more adequate means may be required. When two or more samples are to be collected during one run, several of these interchangeable traps should be available for collecting the eluate under each peak.

Another collecting device can be made from thin-walled glass tubing of suitable length and diameter, for example, melting point glass tubing. The tube is easily slipped into the exit port and the protruding section cooled by solid carbon dioxide. The cooling agent is contained in a small paper cup having opposing holes in its sides for slipping the tubing through it. This is an especially convenient technique for collecting samples for melting point comparison. After collecting the sample, one end of the tube is sealed and the melting point is determined directly, eliminating any need to transfer the sample. There are several methods for identification of a small effluent sample. We have used melting point determinations routinely. Other methods include visible and ultraviolet absorption spectrometry, or infrared and emission spectroscopy. Selection of the appropriate method is in accordance with the sample size available and the sensitivity of the method for the most characteristic property of the sample.

Fractions of the effluents may be collected and reinjected to determine whether or not identical behavior is obtained. A reinjected sample which was partially degraded during the prior run usually produces a different chromatogram from the one originally obtained.

HEALTH HAZARDS

Exposure to an atmosphere containing beryllium compounds often causes severe toxicological reactions. The United States Atomic Energy Commission has recommended a tentative maximum exposure level of 2 μg m^{-3} of beryllium average concentration for an eight hour work day, and 25 μg m^{-3} at a single exposure. In working with beryllium compounds, it is recommended that rubber gloves be worn and work carried out in a well-ventilated fume hood.

No information is available on the toxicity of the fluorocarbon β-diketones or the metal chelates with these ligands. The ligands have very unpleasant and irritating odors and this fact alone suggests that the syntheses should be performed in a fume hood.

Commercial gas chromatographic instruments are not generally equipped with effluent trapping devices. The effluent emerging from the instrument, if not trapped, diffuses throughout the atmosphere of the laboratory. Should metals which may act as cumulative poisons be constantly emptied into the laboratory as volatile metal complexes, a health hazard is likely. For prevention of contamination of the laboratory atmosphere it is advisable to vent gas chromatographic effluent streams to a fume hood, or, if this is not practical, a cold trap should be attached to the exit port of the instrument.

When radioactive nuclides are employed in ionization detectors, or when the sample contains radioactive material the Atomic Energy Commission regulations guarding against accidental spillage and improper handling of such isotopes should be rigorously followed. Tritium radioactive sources, for example, must never be heated above the recommended maximum temperature.

REFERENCES

1. S. Dal Nogare and R. S. Juvet, Jr., *Gas–Liquid Chromatography*, Interscience, New York, 1962.
2. E. Bayer, *Gas Chromatography*, Elsevier, Amsterdam, 1961.
3. A. I. M. Keulemans, *Gas Chromatography*, Reinhold, New York, 1960.
4. A. B. Littlewood, *Gas Chromatography*, Academic Press, New York, 1962.
5. E. Heftmann (Ed.), *Chromatography*, Reinhold, New York, 1961.
6. H. Purnell, *Gas Chromatography*, Wiley, New York, 1962.
7. D. Ambrose and B. A. Ambrose, *Gas Chromatography*, Newnes, London, 1961.
8. J. H. Knox, *Gas Chromatography*, Methuen, London, 1962.
9. S. Claesson, *Arkiv Kemi, Mineral Geol.*, **23A**, 1 (1946).
10. R. E. Sievers, B. W. Ponder, M. L. Morris and R. W. Moshier, *Inorg. Chem.* **2**, 693 (1963).
11. R. E. Sievers, American Chemical Society 16th Annual Summer Symposium on Analytical Chemistry, Tucson, Arizona, June 19, 1963; *Chem. and Eng. News* **41**, 41 (July 1, 1963).
12. R. W. Moshier, J. E. Schwarberg, M. L. Morris and R. E. Sievers, 14th Conference on Analytical Chemistry and Applied Spectroscopy, Pittsburgh, Pa., March 5, 1963.
13. J. E. Schwarberg, Masters Thesis, University of Dayton, 1964; J. E. Schwarberg, R. W. Moshier and J. H. Walsh, *Talanta*, **11**, 1213 (1964).
14. A. A. Duswalt, Jr., Doctoral Dissertation, Purdue University, 1959.
15. W. V. Floutz, Masters Thesis, Purdue University, 1959.
16. R. S. Juvet, Jr. and F. M. Wachi, *Anal. Chem.*, **32**, 290 (1960); F. M. Wachi, Doctoral Dissertation, University of Illinois, 1959.
17. R. A. Keller, *J. Chromatog.*, **5**, 225 (1961).
18. H. W. Myers and R. F. Putnam, *Anal. Chem.*, **34**, 664 (1962).
19. F. Zado, *New Nuclear Materials Including Non-Metallic Fuels*, Vol. II., International Atomic Energy Agency, Vienna, 1963, p. 49.
20. R. A. Keller and H. Freiser, *Gas Chromatography, 1960*, Ed. by R. P. W. Scott, Butterworths, London, 1960, p. 301.
21. A. G. Hamlin, G. Iveson and T. R. Phillips, *Anal. Chem.*, **35**, 2037 (1963), and references cited therein.
22. J. E. Lovelock, *Anal. Chem.*, **33**, 162 (1961), and references cited therein.
23. J. E. Lovelock and S. R. Lipsky, *J. Am. Chem. Soc.*, **82**, 431 (1960).
24. W. D. Ross, *Anal. Chem.*, **35**, 1596 (1963).
25. W. D. Ross and G. Wheeler, Jr., *Anal. Chem.*, **36**, 266 (1964); W. D. Ross, R. E. Sievers and G. Wheeler, Jr., *Anal. Chem.*, **37**, 598 (1965).
26. D. K. Albert, *Anal. Chem.*, **36** 2034, (1964).
27. W. D. Ross, unpublished data.
28. I. G. McWilliam and R. A. Dewar, *Gas Chromatography*, ed. by D. H. Desty, Butterworths, London, 1958.
29. I. G. McWilliam and R. A. Dewar, *Nature* **182**, 1664 (1958).
30. J. Harley, W. Nel and V. Pretorius, *Nature* **181**, 177 (1958).
31. W. W. Brandt and J. E. Heveran, 142nd National Meeting, American Chemical Society, Atlantic City, New Jersey, Sept. 9–14, 1962.
32. J. E. Heveran, Masters Thesis, Purdue University, 1962.
33. R. D. Hill and H. Gesser. *J. Gas Chromatography* **1**, 11 (Oct. 1963).

34. R. D. HILL, Masters Thesis, University of Manitoba, 1962.
35. J. E. LOVELOCK, *J. Chromatog.*, **1**, 35 (1958).
36. W. J. BIERMANN and H. GESSER, *Anal. Chem.*, **32**, 1525 (1960).
37. W. G. BALDWIN, Masters Thesis, University of Manitoba, 1961.
38. S. A. RYCE and W. D. BRYCE, *Nature*, **179**, 541 (1957).
39. R. E. SIEVERS, R. W. MOSHIER and M. L. MORRIS, *Inorg. Chem.*, **1**, 966 (1962).
40. D. W. GRANT, *Gas Chromatography, 1958*, Ed. by D. H. DESTY, Academic Press, New York, 1958, p. 153.
41. J. L. MONKMAN and L. DUBOIS, *Gas Chromatography*, Ed. by H. J. NOE-BELS, R. F. WALL and N. BRENNER, Academic Press, New York, 1961, p. 333.
42. R. S. JUVET and R. DURBIN, *J. Gas Chromatography*, **1**, 14 (Dec. 1963).
43. R. S. JUVET, JR., private communication to R. E. SIEVERS, May 11, 1964.
44. J. F. ELLIS, C. W. FORREST and P. L. ALLEN, *Anal. Chim. Acta*, **22**, 27 (1960).
45. J. F. ELLIS and C. W. FORREST, *J. Inorg. Nucl. Chem.*, **16**, 150 (1960).
46. J. TADMOR, *J. Inorg. Nucl. Chem.*, **23**, 158 (1961); J. TADMOR, *Anal. Chem.*, **36**, 1565 (1964).
47. J. TADMOR, *Research Council of Israel, Bulletin, Chem. Soc.*, **10A**, No. 3 : 17 (Sept. 1961); *ibid*, **11A**, No. 2; 144 (July 1962); J. TADMOR, *J. Gas Chromatography*, **2**, 385, (1964).
48. A. I. M. KEULEMANS, *Gas Chromatography, 1960*, Ed. by R. P. W. SCOTT, Butterworths, 1960, Washington, p. 307.
49. W. Q. HULL, H. KEEL, J. KENNEY and B. W. GAMSON, *Ind. Eng. Chem.*, **45**, 256 (1953).
50. E. C. HORNING, E. A. MOSCATELLI and C. C. SWEELEY, *Chem. and Ind.*, 751 (1959).
51. J. BOHEMEN, S. H. LANGER, R. H. PERRETT and J. H. PURNELL, *J. Chem. Soc.*, 2444 (1960).
52. J. J. KIRKLAND, 14th Conference on Analytical Chemistry and Applied Spectroscopy, Pittsburgh, Pa., March 1963.
53. C. HISHTA, J. P. MESSERLY, R. F. RESCHKE, D. H. FREDERICK and W. D. COOKE, *Anal. Chem.*, **32**, 880 (1960).
54. C. HISHTA, J. P. MESSERLY and R. F. RESCHKE, *Anal. Chem.*, **32**, 1730 (1960).
55. D. H. FREDERICK, B. T. MIRANDA and W. D. COOKE, *Anal. Chem.*, **34**, 1521 (1962).
56. R. E. SIEVERS, B. W. PONDER and R. W. MOSHIER, 141st National Meeting, American Chemical Society, Washington, D.C., March 24, 1962.
57. R. G. LINCK and R. E. SIEVERS, 148th National Meeting, American Chemical Society, Chicago, Ill., Sept. 1964.
58. R. W. MOSHIER, unpublished data.
59. H. FREISER, *Anal. Chem.*, **31**, 1440 (1959).
60. C. P. ELLIS, *Anal. Chem.*, **35**, 1327 (1963).
61. W. W. BRANDT, *Gas Chromatography, 1960*, Ed. by R. P. W. SCOTT, Butterworths, 1960, Washington, p. 305.
62. R. G. MELCHER, Masters Thesis, Purdue University, 1961.

CHAPTER 4

ANALYTICAL DETERMINATIONS

PRELIMINARY OPERATIONS

QUALITATIVE and quantitative determinations of metals by gas chromatography require sample treatment steps that yield volatile metal chelates. Preferably, the chelate should be one which can be used in a solution. Although means are available for inserting solid samples into the apparatus, they are less convenient than injection with the microsyringe which is used when the sample is a liquid, for example, a solution of the metal chelate.

The metal chelate may be prepared by dissolving the sample, adding an excess of the chelating agent to the acidified sample solution, and adjusting the pH to an optimum value. Precipitation of the metal chelate occurs. This method is recommended for preparation of pure samples for exploratory studies. Gas chromatography applied to these precipitates by solid sample-injection is not very practical for quantitative analysis. Considerable time is required to collect the precipitate on a filter and to wash it free from foreign material. Product loss is very probable because of its hydrophobic character and its tendency to adhere to solid objects. However, the precipitate can be dissolved in a water-immiscible solvent and the solvent evaporated to obtain a quantitative recovery of the metal chelate. For gas chromatographic purposes it is preferred to convert the metal content of the sample into a chelate by a method which does not involve precipitation.

Operation in a binary solvent system provides such a method[1]. Reaction of the diketone with the metal salt in aqueous solution is the usual method of preparation resulting in the water-insoluble metal chelate. In some preparations nonaqueous media are necessary. Precipitation of the chelate can be avoided by conducting the reaction in the presence of a solvent for the chelate. The solvent should be water-immiscible and it should be so efficient that the chelate dissolves before it has a chance to appear as a precipitate. Benzene, chloroform, carbon tetrachloride and the chelating agent itself have been found to be very useful solvents. The use of the solvents chloroform and carbon tetrachloride has the advantage of giving the extract a density greater than the aqueous layer, permitting it to be removed first from the extraction funnel. The aqueous phase remains in the funnel for subsequent treatment. Immediate contact of the newly formed chelate with the solvent is realized by adding a solution of the chelating agent in the same solvent. This procedure, with accompanying intimate mixing by agitation, is recommended.

There are several equilibria involved in the system. The reaction conditions should be chosen to favor equilibrium toward formation of the metal chelate. In order to effect this, the following is recommended:

In dissolving the sample prior to formation of the complex, avoid using reagents which possess anions that compete with the chelating agent for the metal. The perchlorate ion does not exhibit an appreciable tendency for complex formation and is therefore quite satisfactory. Some anions, such as nitrate, can be successfully employed as well. Usually the sample contains two or more metals, when it is desirable to obtain the chelate of only selected metals, an auxiliary complexing agent may be added to the solution to prevent formation of the chelates of and the extraction of the undesired metals. At the same time the auxiliary complexing agent must not interfere significantly with the formation and extraction of the diketonates of the desired metals. Buffering agents often are organic acids which may be regarded as auxiliary complexing agents. Therefore, when buffers are used, they should be carefully selected to avoid interference in the extraction process.

The metal chelate should have a high stability constant. It should have a high relative solubility in the organic solvent. A metal β-diketonate of lower stability constant will be transferred to a less extent to the organic phase than one with a higher stability constant. When this is the case the procedure will need to be repeated a number of times to obtain quantitative transfer of the metal chelate to the organic phase.

The β-diketones are in keto–enol equilibria. For ease of complex formation they should possess water solubility. The ease of complex formation is strongly pH dependent because of the competition of the proton for the basic sites on the ligand. Therefore, complex formation is retarded when the solution is more acidic.

Formation of most metal β-diketonates is extremely rapid at ambient temperature. In a few cases the reaction rate is slow and operation at a higher temperature is indicated. For the practical application of solvent extraction, operating conditions should be selected which permit extraction to be effected in a minimum time. In this system addition of an excess of the β-diketone dissolved in the organic phase is desirable. Generally the metal chelate is not transferred quantitatively to the organic phase in one operation because of the relative solubility of the metal chelate in the two liquids. In a very few cases quantitative transfer is so nearly attained that some quantitative analytical methods are based on a one-operation extraction. Very rapid attainment of equilibrium in other cases to a high and reproducible level has permitted one-step extractions to be applied in analytical methods. Very careful control of conditions is necessary in using these procedures. Commercially available extraction funnels equipped with Teflon stopcocks, which do not require lubrication, obviate funnel leakage so prevalent in the use of lubricated glass stopcocks. For theoretical treatments of binary solvent systems the reader is referred to other publications[1–11].

The effect of pH on the reaction is so pronounced that a first requirement in applying the system to the preparation of a metal chelate is a study of efficiency of the extraction as a function of pH. The optimum pH range for the transfer of a metal from the aqueous phase into the organic phase is determined as follows:

Prepare several identical metal salt solutions in which the pH is progressively varied. In turn, contact each solution with an excess of reagent for a definite time, using identical volumes of a stock solution of the reagent in the organic solvent. Determine the amount of metal transferred to the organic phase in each experiment. From these data is obtained the pH range for the largest percentage of metal transferred. The pH of the aqueous layer at equilibrium is the significant value. For application of solvent extraction to new problems a file of these data should be maintained for ready reference.

When equilibrium is attained rather slowly, and time is important, authors have realized the inadvisability of awaiting the attainment of equilibrium. It is better to repeat the process a few times to obtain the required extraction. This requires less time, provided that an appreciable quantity of metal chelate is removed in each step of the operation.

Acetylacetone is the simplest member of the homologous series of β-diketones. The popularity of acetylacetone is undoubtedly due to the great amount of information available on its metal compounds and to its ready availability at reasonable cost. Solvent extraction is admirably applicable to the use of the β-diketones as reagents because they form well-defined chelates with many metals. (See the Appendix, page 138.) Fluorinated β-diketone metal chelates have been much less studied than the acetylacetonates, but for gas chromatographic separations they are of greater interest because of their greater volatility.

Colorimetric methods for metal analysis have relied heavily on the use of solvent extraction for formation and separation of metal chelates. A brief outline of the published studies concerning utilization of the metal acetylacetonates follows.

Starý and Hladký[12] presented data on equilibria in the extraction of metal acetylacetonates by benzene. They found that the extraction equilibrium is established in a very few minutes for all metal acetylacetonates except those of magnesium, molybdenum, cobalt and nickel, which require several hours. The extractability of several metal acetylacetonates by benzene decreases in the following order:
Pd(II), Tl(III), Fe(III), Be(II), Ga(III) and Cu(II), greater than Sc(III), Al(III), In(III), UO$_2$(II), Th(IV), Pb(II), Ni(II), La(III), Co(II) and Zn(II), greater than Mn(II) and Mg(II). Not extracted at pH 0 to >10 are the acetylacetonates of Ca(II), Sr(II), Ba(II), Ag(I), Cd(II) and Bi(III). Data were also obtained for the metal benzoylacetonates and dibenzoylmethanates.

Acetylacetone can serve as both the reactant and solvent in this system. Steinbach and Freiser[13] determined the equilibrium extraction curves for beryllium, copper and zinc acetylacetonates using a sulfuric acid solution of the metals at pH 2.1 (Fig. 4.1). Copper was quantitatively separated from zinc by extracting at pH 2.1. Five to seven repetitions of the process were necessary. These same authors[14] used acetylacetone as both reagent and solvent in the analysis of systems containing aluminum, gallium and indium. In a later study McKaveney and Freiser[15] used acetylacetone as both reagent and solvent in the separation and determination of molybdenum in ferrous materials.

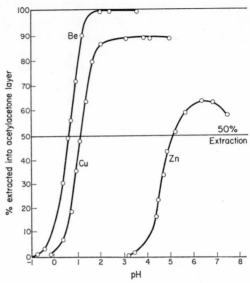

FIG. 4.1. Data obtained on the extraction of metal acetylacetonates from sulfuric acid solution by acetylacetone.
(Courtesy of *Analytical Chemistry*)

McKaveney and Freiser[15] demonstrated that when the chelating agent is dissolved in carbon tetrachloride, the equilibrium is displaced toward the organic phase by increasing the reagent concentration, and that at a concentration of 50 per cent, or greater, 96 per cent of iron is in the organic phase. Abrahamczik[16,17] used this reagent solution in the removal of iron, aluminum and manganese from magnesium. Adam, Booth and Strickland[18] used acetylacetone dissolved in chloroform in the presence of EDTA for the isolation and determination of beryllium. Kenny, Maton and Spragg[19] found that the reagent dissolved in xylene is excellent for the selective separation of radioactive iron-59 from cobalt in the pH 4.0–7.0 range. Acetylacetone as a reagent dissolved in benzene was applied to the isolation of protactinium by

Maddock and Miles[20]. Toribara and Chen[21] applied this reagent solution to the isolation of beryllium from urine. The sample, wet-ashed with nitric–sulfuric acid, was first electrolyzed to remove interfering metals. The resulting solution, adjusted to pH 4.5, was then contacted with the reagent solution. Krishen and Freiser[22] used acetylacetone as a reagent dissolved in benzene in the determination of the effect of the presence of EDTA on the isolation of uranium, copper, lead and bismuth. (Figures 4.2a and 4.2b.) The efficiency of the extraction of copper and bismuth was diminished by the presence of EDTA. For isolation of uranyl acetylacetonate no large change in the efficiency was apparent. However, in the presence of EDTA the efficiency peak had shifted from $pH_{\frac{1}{2}}$* 1.65 to $pH_{\frac{1}{2}}$ 2.25.

Other separation studies applying solvent extraction and utilizing β-diketones have been reported as follows:

of beryllium with acetylacetone at pH 5–10, by Bolomey and Broido[23]; of plutonium(IV) with acetylacetone, trifluoroacetylacetone, and benzoylacetone at pH 2–10, by Harvey, Heal, Maddock and Rowley[24]; of uranium(VI) with dibenzoylmethane, by Pribil and Jelinek[25], and Rydberg[26]; and of thorium at pH above 5.8, by Rydberg[27].

Crandall and Thomas[28] studied the separation of zirconium from mixtures containing the metals, zirconium, niobium, rare earths, and alkaline earths, utilizing 0.01–0.03 M solutions in organic solvents of fluorine derivatives of beta-diketones of the general formula $RC(:0)CH_2C(:0)C(R')(F)(R'')$, in which R is an alkyl, aryl, aralkyl, or heterocyclic radical, and R' and R'' are H or F. Thenoyltrifluoroacetone, benzoyltrifluoroacetone, and trifluoroacetylacetone were preferred.

The knotty problem of zirconium and hafnium separation has been studied by Connick and McVey[29], who applied solvent extraction using thenoyltrifluoroacetone dissolved in benzene. These investigators found that perchloric, hydrochloric, and nitric acids, even at 2 M concentration, were satisfactory media because zirconium is complexed only weakly in these acids as compared to solutions containing sulfuric or hydrofluoric acids. Huffman and

---

* $pH_{\frac{1}{2}}$ is defined as the value at which 50 per cent of the metal is transferred to the organic phase.

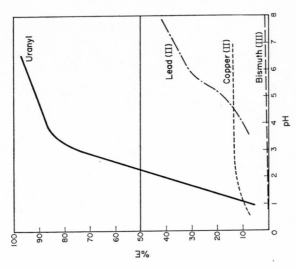

FIG. 4.2b. Extraction of acetylacetonates by acetylacetone in presence of (ethylenedinitrilo) tetraacetic acid.

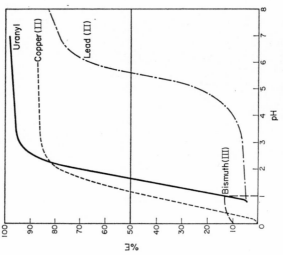

FIG. 4.2a. Extraction of acetylacetonates by acetylacetone.

(Courtesy of *Analytical Chemistry*)

Beaufait[30] also used the binary solvent system with thenoyltri-fluoroacetone dissolved in benzene and 2 M perchloric acid for the zirconium–hafnium solution. They were able to separate the two metals partially. An extension of this study by Schultz and Larsen[31] resulted in a successful separation of zirconium and hafnium. The extraction was accomplished by contacting a benzene solution of trifluoroacetylacetone with a 1.5 M hydrochloric acid solution of the metals. The tetrakis (1,1,1-trifluoro-2,4-pentanedionato)zirconium(IV) compound, thus formed, was preferentially transferred to the organic phase. Most of the hafnium remained in the aqueous phase because the greater stability of the chloro complex suppressed chelate formation. The efficiency of the separation is affected by the diketone concentration, metal concentration, and hydrochloric acid concentration.

In another study illustrating the value of trifluoroacetylacetone, Crandall, Thomas and Reid[32] found this reagent valuable in the isolation of plutonium(IV).

Moshier[33a] made a preliminary examination of the use of trifluoroacetylacetone as reagent in the application of the binary solvent system. Quantitative formation and transfer into benzene, chloroform, or carbon tetrachloride was obtained for aluminum and iron as their tris-β-diketonates at pH 3.0 and for copper bis-β-diketonate at pH 4.2. These three solvents were unsuited for the isolation of nickel and cobalt because they wetted but did not dissolve the metal chelates. At pH 5.7 the nickel and cobalt chelates were formed and quantitatively extracted into n-hexanol or amyl acetate as solvents. Nickel and cobalt were not detectable in the aqueous phase. Scribner[33], using 0.1 M trifluoroacetylacetone, b.p. 106–107°C, in alcohol-free chloroform, described a quantitative study of the application of solvent extraction to the preparation of metal trifluoroacetylacetonates. Over the pH range 4–8, 99 per cent of copper(II), initially 0.001 M, was rapidly removed from the aqueous medium. Over the pH range 4–7, 98 per cent of aluminum, initially 0.001 M, was removed from the aqueous medium. An equilibration time of ten minutes was required. At pH 2.3, 99.5 per cent of iron (III), initially 0.001 M, was rapidly and quantitatively removed from the aqueous medium. Iron(III) in aqueous media below pH 2.3 requires much longer equilibration time to attain this efficiency. In this study equal volumes of organic and aqueous phases were used.

In gas chromatography the choice of solvent is important. It is desirable to have a highly volatile solvent for the metal chelate in order to obtain rapid elution with little or no tailing of its chromatographic peak. When the solvent is eluted first (as is the usual case), if the peak tails, early eluted solute peaks often appear as shoulders on the tail of the solvent peak. This causes difficulty in the measurement of peak areas. Brandt and Heveran[34,35] found carbon disulfide satisfactory for extracting chromium(III) acetyl-acetonate, and superior to other solvents in the gas chromatographic determination of the chelate because the flame ionization detector used for the study was insensitive to carbon disulfide. Therefore, it did not interfere seriously with the determination.

Ross and Wheeler[36] used the solvent toluene, which was eluted subsequent to the metal chelate in the gas chromatography of chromium(III) hexafluoroacetylacetonate. Toluene was retained by the column long enough that it did not interfere with the detection of the chromium complex or the chloroform which was used as an internal standard.

Chloroform has been found to form addition compounds with some metal β-diketonates, according to Steinbach and Burns[37]. They state that chloroform is so weakly bonded to the metal chelate (by van der Waals forces) that it is readily removed at elevated temperatures.

PREPARATION OF tfa, hfa AND ANHYDROUS CHLORIDE COMPLEXES OF METALS

Metal trifluoroacetylacetonates are readily prepared from aqueous solutions of the metals. Schultz and Larsen[38] have shown that the metal chelates of hexafluoroacetylacetone, however, are often not easily prepared in aqueous solutions because of the readiness of the ketone to form dihydrates. In an organic solvent such as ethanol reaction is much easier. Several anhydrous metal chlorides and bromides readily react with hexafluoroacetylacetone providing a convenient method for preparing the complexes. The extent of displacement of the halogen of the metal halide is dependent upon the temperature of the reaction mixture and the oxidation state of the metal[39]. Commercially supplied hexa-fluoroacetylacetone[40] contains a small quantity of the dihydrate of the ketone and it must be rendered anhydrous for quantitative use by shaking it with two portions of sulfuric acid (d 1.84) in a separatory funnel.

For the preparation of anhydrous metal halides from the metal oxides Tyree[41] discusses five classes of methods: (1) dehydration of hydrated salts; (2) direct synthesis; (3) reaction of metal oxide— method is limited to the preparation of the chlorides and bromides; (4) displacement reactions; (5) special reactions, (examples are decomposition of higher-valent halide at an elevated temperature to produce the lower-valent metal halide, vanadium(III) chloride by treating vanadium powder with iodine mono-chloride, thermal decomposition of zirconium oxychloride, rare earth chlorides by extracting the metal benzoate wtih an ether solution of hydrogen chloride).

Class (3) is the one best suited to the quantitative conversion of many metal oxides to the metal chloride or metal bromide. Atkinson, Steigman, and Hiskey[42] converted niobium and tantalum oxides to the pentachlorides in an apparatus of special design by refluxing with octachloropropane under anhydrous conditions. To obtain quantitative results a preliminary separation of iron was required.

A much simpler method of preparing metal chlorides was developed by Camboulives[43]. He converted 33 metal oxides to the chlorides by treating them with carbon tetrachloride. Boron trioxide and silicon dioxide do not undergo this reaction. Elements which form volatile oxychlorides are converted to this product when carbon tetrachloride vapor is passed through a heated tube containing the metal oxide. The fully chlorinated compound can be obtained by performing the reaction in a sealed tube containing an excess of carbon tetrachloride. A safe method for conducting sealed glass tube reactions was presented by Knox, Tyree, Srivastava, Norman, Bassett and Holloway[44]. They placed a weighed quantity of metal oxide into the tube and added carbon tetrachloride in at least a five-fold excess. They used 8 ml of carbon tetrachloride for every 26 ml of volume of the tube after sealing. The sealed tube was placed in a cylindrical metal bomb. To equalize the external and internal pressures, they added 8 ml of carbon tetrachloride for every 26 ml of free space remaining in the bomb. In this way the reaction tube was not fractured during the synthesis. They heated the bomb for a few hours in a tube furnace at 300–400°C, the temperature depending upon the reaction characteristics of the charge. Reaction by-products consisted of phosgene, solid chlorocarbons, and sometimes chlorine.

Refractory oxides were inert in this process if they had been ignited to a high temperature. For these oxides conversion of the metal oxide to the activated form by dissolution, precipitation, and ignition of the hydrated oxide at low temperature was recommended. Incomplete conversion of zinc, lanthanum and thorium oxides to the chlorides was believed to be due to the relatively non-volatile properties of the chlorides. For the preparation of anhydrous metal bromides, carbon tetrabromide or bromoform were suitable reagents.

In a later study Bardawil, Collier and Tyree[45] applied this method to the preparation of anhydrous metal chlorides from the metal sulfides of tungsten, molybdenum, rhenium, and iron. When the sulfide was an ore, unreacted acid-insoluble residues remained.

Procedure for Preparing Metal Hexafluoroacetylacetonates from Anhydrous Metal Chlorides[39]

Preparation of the Reaction Tube. Prepare borosilicate reaction tubes 18–20 cm in length from tubing 1.3 cm o.d. and 1.0 cm i.d. and seal at one end. The reaction tubes were cleaned and dried at 130°C, and stored in a desiccator. To carry out a preparation, weigh the tube, add the ignited metal oxide (using not more than 0.20 g), reweigh the tube and place it in an upright position, add 0.80–1.00 ml of carbon tetrachloride (dried over phosphorous pentoxide), place the tube upright in a container of solid carbon dioxide (Dry Ice), seal the open end making certain that the seal is uniform and without thin spots, and remove the tube from the cold bath.

Preparation of the Metal Chloride

After the tube has reached room temperature place it in a cold, multiple unit, hinged type, combustion furnace regulated by a rheostat. After inserting a thermocouple close the ends of the furnace with glass wool. Bring the temperature of the furnace up slowly during about a one hour period. Tubes placed in a hot furnace tend to fracture, with loss of the preparation and damage to the heater. The reaction is complete when inspection shows no residue of unreacted metal oxides, provided, of course, that the metal chloride is gaseous at the furnace temperature. Turn off the furnace, open the hinged top, pick up the tube with casserole tongs, and stand it upright in a beaker. The metal chloride condenses first, followed by the excess carbon tetrachloride which rinses down the wall of the tube. One and one-half to three hours are required for this procedure. Eye protection is mandatory throughout.

Ferric chloride prepared in this manner crystallizes from the vapor state in platelets and may not rinse down with the condensed carbon tetrachloride. When solid remains on the walls, care should be exercised in opening the tube and in treating both sections of the tube with the β-diketone. Titanium tetrachloride usually remains completely dissolved in the carbon tetrachloride after the tube has cooled to ambient temperature. The solubilities of the chlorides of niobium, tantalum, molybdenum, and tungsten are low and crystallization occurs upon cooling.

Preparation of the Metal Hexafluoroacetylacetonate

When the tube has reached room temperature, stand it upright in a short Dewar flask containing Dry Ice and transfer it to a dry box, dehydrated with phosphorus pentoxide. After the carbon tetrachloride has frozen, remove the tube from the flask, cut it near the mid-section with a file or glass cutter and snap it in two. Place the section containing the products back into the Dry Ice. Measure out 1 ml, a liberal excess, of hexafluoroacetylacetone and pour it into the tube containing the cold metal chloride. Remove the tube from the Dry Ice and warm it with the gloved fingers. After the carbon tetrachloride has melted, reaction starts and hydrogen chloride bubbles evolve at a rate governed by the temperature. (Caution: titanium tetrachloride is very soluble in carbon tetrachloride and this solution reacts vigorously with hexafluoroacetylacetone. Add the reagent drop-by-drop to these carbon tetrachloride solutions of titanium tetrachloride). The reaction is complete on cessation of hydrogen chloride evolution. Surrounding the tube with a cooling bath and heating to reflux temperature removes hydrogen chloride and promotes completion of chelation of some metals. For example, at room temperature the monochelate of niobium is formed. Under reflux temperature conditions, there is a slow conversion to the tri-chelated compound. Any solid residue or turbidity is due either to impurities or incomplete conversion residues of the metal oxide. Pour the solution into a dry calibrated 2 ml container and rinse off the hanging drop with carbon tetrachloride using a small squeeze bottle fitted with a flexible capillary tube. A convenient bottle and tube is that supplied with Gas Chromatographic Sampljectors[46]. Rinse the tube at least five times with small portions of carbon tetrachloride, transferring the rinsings to the main solution. Dilute to volume with additional carbon tetrachloride and mix. Solutions containing moisture-sensitive compounds may be transferred to ampoules for later gas chromatographic use. One-half to one hour is required for this procedure.

To obtain the pure metal chelate, for example the hexafluoroacetylacetonato niobium(V) chelate for characterization, one may transfer the reaction product mixture from the reaction tube to a suitable closed distillation vessel and distill off the excess carbon tetrachloride and β-diketone under reduced pressure at ambient temperature. A water pump is convenient when provided with an intervening Dry Ice trap. The niobium chelate can then be distilled at 35–60°C/2 mm in a molecular still. The hexafluoroacetylacetonates of iron(III), titanium(IV) niobium(V), tantalum(V), molybdenum(V), tungsten(VI) and trifluoroacetylacetonates of zirconium and hafnium have been prepared by this method.

GAS CHROMATOGRAPH CONSIDERATIONS FOR VOLATILE, MOISTURE-SENSITIVE HEXAFLUORO-ACETYLACETONATES OF TITANIUM, NIOBIUM AND TANTALUM

Because of their moisture-sensitivity, the sampling and gas chromatographic injection of carbon tetrachloride solutions of the hexafluoroacetylacetonates of titanium, niobium, and tantalum was conducted in a dry chamber fitted to the F & M Model 500 instrument. The dry chamber consisted of a transparent Glove Bag[47]. The inert gas inlet tube of the bag was enlarged so as to fit snugly over a cork stopper and held in place with a rubber band. The cork stopper was hollowed out to fit tightly around the hexagonal septum retainer of the gas chromatograph injection port. To shape the Glove Bag a rigid frame was constructed from Flexaframe rods inside the bag. A Petri dish containing phosphorus pentoxide was kept inside the bag to maintain the chamber moisture-free.

The carbon tetrachloride solutions of the samples were contained in 1-dram vials. A micro-syringe was used to introduce the sample.

Initial determinations of the gas chromatographic behavior of the chloro-hexafluoroacetylacetonates of titanium(IV), tantalum(V) and niobium(V) were made using products purified in a molecular still. Later, the crude reaction products, obtained by the described procedure, gave identical chromatograms. The chromatogram for the tantalum compound contained very small peaks attributed to the presence of titanium and niobium impurities. Likewise, the chromatogram for the niobium compound contained small peaks attributed to the presence of titanium and tantalum. A crude reaction product mixture of the titanium, tantalum and niobium compounds was studied to obtain conditions for good resolution. By applying temperature programming the separation shown in Fig. 4.3 was obtained.

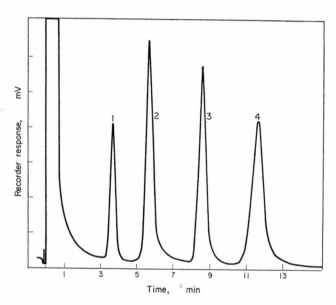

FIG. 4.3. Chromatogram of 1, $TiCl_4$; 2, $TiCl_2(hfa)_2$; 3, $TaCl_3(hfa)_2$; 4, $NbCl_4(hfa)$. Helium flow 79 ml min^{-1}; temperature programmed at 5.9°C min^{-1} from 55 to 74°C. *Column:* 61 cm long, 4 mm i.d. of borosilicate glass filled with 5 per cent by weight Dow Corning High Vacuum Grease coated on 60–80 mesh Chromosorb W. *Retention time:* 1, 3.8 min; 2, 5.8 min; 3, 8.7 min; 4, 11.7 min.

Necessary Observations in the Gas Chromatography of Metal Chelates

Thermal stability of the metal chelate at the column operating temperature is required before quantitative data can be obtained. When one or more metal chelates in a sample decompose, early peaks produced by volatile degradation products may render the chromatogram meaningless. Thermal degradation is generally greater in the injection port than in the column because the port is held at the higher temperature. Chelates which escape decomposition in the port can, however, decompose in the column. Volatile degradation products produced in the column cause anomalous baseline changes which are superimposed on other peaks obtained from the other metal chelates present in the sample, so that interpretative measurements of these latter compounds becomes difficult. It is advisable to determine the thermal stability of each of the anticipated metal chelates in early exploratory studies. Interchangeable glass inserts in the injection port served admirably in this exploratory study (see Chapter 3). The glass liner was removed periodically and examined for deposits.

Polymerization of the degradation products or of the chelate sample itself may take place. Hence, appearance of either unexpected peaks or of deposits should be viewed with caution and investigated. The accuracy of the gas chromatographic analysis of the metal chelates depends, of course, upon the complete elution of the unaltered sample. Non-volatile materials resulting from thermal or solvolytic decomposition of samples alter the partitioning property of the column, and subsequent information obtained by its later use may be rendered meaningless.

Positive identification of the material producing a peak is made by condensing the material from the effluent gas at the time the peak is formed and by making confirmatory tests on the condensate. For this purpose loosely fitting, oversize, melting point tubing inserted in the exit port with the protruding section cooled by solid carbon dioxide (Dry Ice) for collection of the condensate serves well. In the qualitative analysis of an unknown by gas chromatography, one sometimes finds that retention times are very similar for two or more compounds. Therefore, a file of retention data for all metal chelates is a prime requisite. As an illustration of this point your attention is directed to Fig. 4.4 in which the peaks for the trifluoroacetylacetonates of thallium, beryllium, aluminum, gallium and indium appear in sequence. However, the retention times for the trifluoroacetylacetonates of copper(II), chromium(III) and iron(III) are almost identical with that of indium when obtained under the same operating conditions. The indium, or copper(II), etc., peaks obtained at this retention time should be viewed with suspicion and confirmatory tests made on a collected sample to assure the analyst of the identity of the compound.

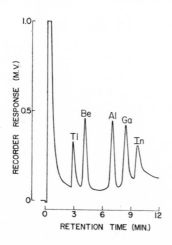

Fig. 4.4. The partial separation of the thallium compound, beryllium(II), aluminum(III), gallium(III) and indium(III) trifluoroacetylacetonates using column 1. The column temperature was programmed from 85 to 160°C at the rate of 7.9°C min⁻¹. A W-1 tungsten detector filament was used.

Specific Retention Volume

Information obtained on the gas chromatography of metal chelates should be recorded in sufficient detail so that the work can be duplicated. The specific retention volumes, or the retention volumes with respect to the air peak or to a well-established standard material are preferred information. These data should include the kind of detector, kind of carrier gas and its flow rate, the column material and dimensions, kind and quantity of solid support the kind and quantity of stationary phase, and the column temperature. The data are obtained at a constant temperature. Data obtained by temperature programming are variable and render calculations of retention volumes meaningless. The uncorrected retention volume is the volume of carrier gas measured from the time of sample injection to the time when the peak maximum has been reached. The uncorrected flow rate is usually obtained using a soap-film flowmeter. The specific retention volume is the corrected volume of carrier gas adjusted to standard temperature and pressure per gram of liquid phase.

The equation for the calculation of specific retention volume is

$$V_g = \left[\frac{3}{2}\frac{[(p_i/p_a)^2 - 1]}{[(p_i/p_a)^3 - 1]}\right] \left[\frac{[FT_c[1 - (p_w/p_a)]]}{T_a}\right] \frac{(t_r - t_a)}{W_L} \frac{273}{T_a}$$

which reduces to

$$V_g = j\left[F_c(t_r - t_a)\frac{1}{W_L}\right]\frac{273}{T_a}$$

where

V_g = specific retention volume.
F = measured flow rate in cubic centimeters of gas per minute, as determined by the soap bubble method.
$F_c = F\frac{T_c}{T_a}[1 - (p_w/p_a)]$
W_L = weight in grams of stationary phase present in the column.
t_r = elapsed time in minutes from injection to sample peak maximum.
t_a = elapsed time in minutes from injection to air peak maximum.
T_c = column temperature in °K.
T_a = room temperature in °K.
p_w = vapor pressure of water at room temperature.
p_a = barometric pressure in the laboratory.
p_i = sum of barometric pressure and gauge pressure of the reduction valve on the carrier gas cylinder; i.e. the inlet pressure of the carrier gas. (Note: Pressures may be expressed in any unit, since they appear as ratios.)

$1 - \dfrac{p_w}{p_a}$ = correction of the wet gas flow-rate as measured by the soap bubble method, to the dry gas flow-rate.

$j = 3/2\dfrac{[(p_i/p_a)^2 - 1]}{[(p_i/p_a)^3 - 1]}$ = compressibility factor, which corrects for the gas pressure drop in the column.

The chromatographic peak for a large sample has a longer apparent retention time than for a small sample due to peak broadening. In determining the specific retention volume it is necessary to obtain chromatograms for several sample injections and extrapolate t_r to zero sample size. The specific retention volume obtained from these data is valid at a given temperature (it is a function of column temperature) for the particular stationary phase on the particular solid support. Any change in one or both alters the value and necessitates a new determination.

A comprehensive treatment of retention has been presented by Dal Nogare and Juvet[48].

QUANTITATIVE DETERMINATIONS

The results of a quantitative gas chromatographic study for the determination of beryllium in a beryllium–copper alloy, made by Baldwin[49], show that the determination of beryllium as the acetylacetonate gave results which differed from the theoretical value for the alloy by 5.3 per cent relative. The beryllium calibration curve, using peak areas, showed a maximum deviation of ± 5.0 per cent. Sources of error realized by Baldwin were incomplete conversion of the beryllium of the sample to its acetylacetonate and sample retention in the micropipette.

This study was made using a Pye Argon Chromatograph equipped with an ionization detector. The 4 ft $\times \frac{1}{4}$ in. borosilicate column was packed with 0.5 per cent by weight Apiezon L grease supported on 200μ glass microbeads. The chromatograms were obtained with the column held at 100°C using an argon flow rate of 50 ml min^{-1}. The peaks were sharp and symmetrical.

In an investigation of the quantitative gas chromatographic analysis of metal β-diketonates Hill and Gesser[50] compared the acetylacetonates, trifluoroacetylacetonates and hexafluoroacetylacetonates of beryllium, aluminum, and chromium.

Operating Conditions

Instrument: Wilkens Aerograph, Model A-600 gas chromatograph equipped with a hydrogen flame ionization detector.
Purified hydrogen flow rate: 30 ml min^{-1}.

Purified air flow rate: 400 ml min^{-1}.
Carrier gas: nitrogen.
Injection block heater: 25–50°C above column temperature.
Hamilton syringe: 10 μl.
Columns: copper tubing, 1–5 ft long, $\frac{1}{8}$ in. o.d., 0.06 in. i.d., packed with 7.5 per cent by weight SE-30 (a methyl silicone polymer) on 40 to 60-mesh fire brick.

Results. The three metal acetylacetonates were chromatographed on a one foot column at 165°C. Linear response was obtained with varying sample sizes for each compound. Of the calibration curves only that of the aluminum compound passed through the origin. The three metal trifluoroacetylacetonates were chromatographed on a one foot column at 106°C with results similar to the metal acetylacetonates. The metal hexafluoroacetylacetonates were chromatographed on a five foot column at 50°C. The longer column was necessary in order to resolve the beryllium and aluminum peaks. The results were similar to those obtained for the metal acetylacetonates. Typical chromatograms are shown for mixtures of the three metal compounds for the acetylacetonates in Fig. 3.5, for the trifluoroacetylacetonates in Fig. 2.8, and for the hexafluoroacetylacetonates in Fig. 2.11.

Quantitative calibration curves were prepared for the metal acetylacetonates and their fluoro-derivatives. A 10 μl. syringe was flushed several times with the standard solution, filled beyond the desired volume, brought to the desired volume, the needle tip wiped, the sample injected. Each calibration point was the average of at least five determinations, with peak areas measured with a planimeter. A known solution of a mixture of the three metal trifluoroacetylacetonates was then analyzed. It was concluded that the analyses are qualitative within an error of ten per cent for quantities as low as 3×10^{-8} mole of metal.

The application of the gas chromatographic method to metal analysis can give much greater accuracy than that shown by the above work of Hill and Gesser. The studies made by Brandt, Ross and Schwarberg, which are described in the subsequent pages, show considerably greater accuracy attainment and typify the present status of the art.

The feasibility of chromium determination by the gas chromato-graphic method was demonstrated by Heveran[34], and Brandt and Heveran[35]. The chromium in aqueous solution was converted to the chromium(III) acetylacetonate and extracted into carbon disulfide. An aliquot of the carbon disulfide solution was injected into the instrument. Considerable tailing of both the solvent and the chelate peak does not permit the presence of other metal chelates whose retention times are near. This was borne out by the interferences due to the presence of beryllium and iron chelates. Therefore a preliminary step for removal of these elements was required.

Instrument Operating Conditions

Instrument: Perkin–Elmer Vapor Fractometer, Model 154-C.
Detector: Perkin–Elmer Flame Ionization Detector 154-0410.
Column: 86 cm long by 4 mm o.d. filled with 80–120 mesh glass beads coated with 0.25 per cent by weight, Silicone oil.
Injection port temperature: 345°C.
Column temperature: 145°C.
Nitrogen flow: 32 ml min^{-1} at 20 psi pressure.
Air flow: 30 ml min^{-1}.
Hydrogen pressure: 25 psi.
Hamilton syringe: 10 μl. capacity. In order to use a 10 μl. sample without putting out the flame of the detector, the hydrogen reduction valve was replaced by one which gave a higher inlet pressure.

Procedure. Transfer an aliquot of the sample solution containing from 0.1 to 10 mg of chromium to a small conical flask and adjust its volume to 10 ml. Extracts from aqueous chromium solutions of concentration below 0.0005 mg ml^{-1} of chromium will yield no chromatographic peak by this procedure. Add a glass bead and bring the solution to boiling, and boil for several minutes to form the more reactive hexaquo complex. Remove the flask from the heater and add an excess of acetylacetone. Adjust the pH of the solution to 9 with 1 M sodium hydroxide solution and mix thoroughly. Boil the resulting mixture for three to five minutes and then cool it to room temperature. Avoid a higher chromium con-centration because serious bumping occurs when the solution is boiled. Add 1.00 ml of carbon disulfide to the flask and agitate thoroughly to transfer the chromium chelate to the carbon disulfide extractant.

Remove the interfering metal chelates of beryllium, aluminum, and iron by a few washings of the carbon disulfide solution with 10 per cent hydrochloric acid solution. This can be accomplished in the conical flask or in a separatory funnel. Bring the small droplets of carbon disulfide to a single globule by inserting the needle of the microsyringe into the organic phase and moving it about. If this is not done erratic results will be obtained. Take a 10 μl. sample with a 10 μl. Hamilton syringe and inject it in the port of the instrument. Determine the chromium content of the sample by comparing the chromatographic peak area to the calibration curve.

Calibration Curve. Dissolve 1.4212 g of potassium dichromate, reagent grade, in 60 ml of water. Add concentrated acids as follows: 10 ml nitric acid, 20 ml hydrochloric acid, and 10 ml sulfuric acid. Evaporate the mixture and heat to evolution of sulfuric acid fumes. Make up the resulting chromic sulfate solution with water to 100 ml in a volumetric flask. The solution contains 4.0 mg ml^{-1} of chromium. Prepare 100 ml volumes each of a series of dilute standard solutions in increments from 0.01 to 1.00 mg ml^{-1} of chromium.

Take 10 ml aliquots of each standard solution and, in the manner described in the procedure, prepare and extract the chromium complex. Omit the step for removing the interfering elements. Obtain the chromatograms for each 10 μl. injection of the carbon disulfide solutions. Plot peak areas versus mg of chromium. In the range 0.1 to 10 mg chromium the calibration curve is linear.

Peak areas: The chromium acetylacetonate peak occurs as a shoulder on the tail of the solvent peak. To obtain the best base line draw a straight line from the start of the chromium peak tangent to the tail of the chromium peak as illustrated in Fig. 3.9. Peak areas were obtained using a K & E Compensating Polar Planimeter, Model 4242, with an accuracy of one part in a thousand.

The non-linear rapid decrease in sensitivity below a concentration of 0.01 mg ml^{-1} chromium does not permit quantitative measurements at this low concentration.

The method was tested by analysis of National Bureau of Standards chromium–molybdenum steel No. 135 with the following results:

Certified: 5.15 per cent chromium.

Found: 5.32 per cent chromium.

Progressively changing from the thermal conductivity detector, to the flame ionization detector, to the electron capture detector renders instrumentation increasingly more sensitive for the detection of eluted metal chelates. By use of an electron capture detector Ross[51] found the limit of detection of chromium(III) hexafluoroacetylacetonate to be 3.3×10^{-11} g, and of aluminum(III) hexafluoroacetylacetonate to be 4.8×10^{-10} g. The sensitivity of the detector is greatest to compounds having high fluorine content in the ligand.

Instrumentation:

Instrument: Barber Colman Model 20 gas chromatograph.
Detector: Ionization detector Model A-4150 with cell potential reduced to less than 200 V, ^{90}Sr radiation source.
Hamilton 10 μl. syringe.

Columns. Two feet and eleven feet long by $\frac{1}{8}$ in. o.d. stainless steel tubing packed with 20 per cent by weight of Dow Corning Silicone Fluid 710R on Gas Chrom Z.

Samples. Aluminum(III) and chromium(III) acetylacetonates, trifluoro-acetylacetonates, and hexafluoroacetylacetonates. Sample solutions, 10–15 mg, dissolved in toluene and made up to 5.00 ml in volumetric flasks. Three consecutive 1 : 25 5-ml dilutions were made for sample injection standards. Sample injection volumes ranged from 0.2 to 10 μl. Toluene was selected as the solvent because it was eluted subsequent to the metal chelates in some cases.

Eluting Gases. Nitrogen or argon.

Procedure. Inject the sample solution and hold the syringe needle in the injection port for 20 sec to permit complete vaporization. Condition the column to the sample by successively chromatogramming six 1 μl. samples of 1×10^{-3} g ml^{-1} concentration; thus reproducible peak heights of subsequent chromatograms are then assured. Use an injection port temperature, 165°C, to cause rapid and total vaporization of the sample. With the optimum conditions determined the peaks obtained are sharp, symmetrical, and reproducible.

Typical chromatograms using argon as carrier gas are shown in Fig. 4.5 for aluminum hexafluoroacetylacetonate, in Fig. 4.6 for chromium hexafluoroacetylacetonate, and in Fig. 2.10 for a mixture of aluminum and chromium hexafluoroacetylacetonates. Substantially greater sensitivity can be achieved using nitrogen carrier gas. Table 4.1 shows the instrument conditions used. Table 4.2 shows the lower detection limits obtained for the six metal chelates in this study. Recently even lower detection limits have been established for some of the complexes[52,59].

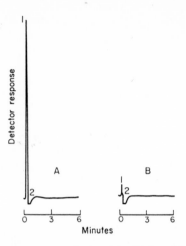

FIG. 4.5. Chromatograms of A: 1.2×10^{-7} g Al(hfa)₃; B: 3.0×10^{-8} g Al(hfa)₃. *Column temperature:* 90°; *Inlet pressure:* 50 psig; *Scavenge flow:* 300 ml min⁻¹. *Cell voltage:* 15 V. (Courtesy of *Analytical Chemistry*)

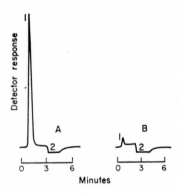

FIG. 4.6. Chromatograms of A: 5.2×10^{-8} g Cr(hfa)₃; B: 8.3×10^{-10} g Cr(hfa)₃. *Column temperature:* 95°. *Inlet pressure:* 20 psig. *Scavenge flow:* 200 ml min⁻¹. *Cell voltage:* 20 V. (Courtesy of *Analytical Chemistry*)

TABLE 4.1. INSTRUMENT CONDITIONS USED IN INVESTIGATION*

Compound	Inlet pressure (psig)	Scavenge flow (ml min^{-1})	Cell voltage	Column temp. (°C)
	Nitrogen eluent			
Cr(acac)$_3$	50	100	25	215
Al(acac)$_3$	50	300	40	185
Cr(tfa)$_3$	24	200	20	162
Al(tfa)$_3$	24	250	30	162
Cr(hfa)$_3$	40	200	15	90
Al(hfa)$_3$	40	200	15	90
	Argon eluent			
Cr(acac)$_3$	20	240	20	215
Al(acac)$_3$	20	100	16	185
Cr(tfa)$_3$	22	75	20	175
Al(tfa)$_3$	22	200	25	160
Cr(hfa)$_3$	20	200	20	95
Al(hfa)$_3$	50	300	15	95

* Courtesy of *Analytical Chemistry*.

TABLE 4.2. LOWER DETECTION LIMITS DETERMINED
FOR ALUMINUM AND CHROMIUM CHELATES*

Compound	Sample size (μl.)	Sample concn. (g ml^{-1})	Peak height (mm)	Signal/noise ratio	Amt. sample detected (g)	Amt. metal detected (moles)
		Nitrogen eluent				
Cr(acac)$_3$	5.0	1.76×10^{-5}	10	10/1	8.8×10^{-8}	2.5×10^{-10}
Cr(tfa)$_3$	1.0	8.96×10^{-8}	4	4/1	9.0×10^{-11}	1.8×10^{-13}
Cr(hfa)$_3$	0.4	8.32×10^{-8}	7	7/1	3.3×10^{-11}	4.9×10^{-14}
Al(acac)$_3$	5.0	1.02×10^{-2}	17	17/1	5.1×10^{-5}	1.6×10^{-7}
Al(tfa)$_3$	1.0	2.68×10^{-6}	2	2/1	2.7×10^{-9}	5.9×10^{-12}
Al(hfa)$_3$	1.0	4.8×10^{-7}	2	2/1	4.8×10^{-10}	7.4×10^{-13}
		Argon eluent				
Cr(acac)$_3$	10.0	1.76×10^{-5}	5	5/1	1.8×10^{-7}	5.0×10^{-10}
Cr(tfa)$_3$	0.1	2.24×10^{-6}	5	5/1	2.2×10^{-10}	4.4×10^{-13}
Cr(hfa)$_3$	0.4	2.08×10^{-6}	5	5/1	8.3×10^{-10}	1.2×10^{-12}
Al(acac)$_3$	0.5	2.1×10^{-2}	10	10/1	1.1×10^{-5}	3.2×10^{-8}
Al(tfa)$_3$	0.2	6.7×10^{-5}	9	9/1	1.3×10^{-8}	2.8×10^{-11}
Al(hfa)$_3$	1.0	4.8×10^{-6}	8	8/1	4.8×10^{-9}	7.4×10^{-12}

* Courtesy of *Analytical Chemistry*.

The quantitative application of the electron capture detector for the determination of chromium as the hexafluoroacetylacetonate by Ross and Wheeler[36] was made over the range 10^{-8} to 10^{-3} g ml^{-1} of the metal chelate. Two calibration curves requiring changes in operating conditions of the instrument were necessary to cover this range. These calibration curves are shown in Fig. 4.7

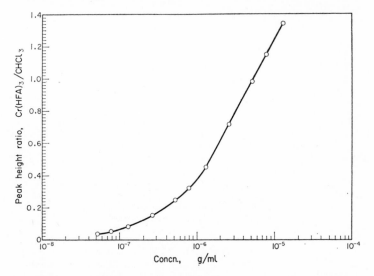

FIG. 4.7. Calibration curve 5.2×10^{-8} to 1.3×10^{-5} g ml^{-1} Cr(hfa)₃. *Column:* 11 ft, *Temperature:* 90°. *Flash heater:* 170°. *Detector:* 200°. *Pressure:* 40 psig. *Split flow:* 75 ml min^{-1}. *Scavenge.* 200 ml min^{-1}. *Electrometer gain:* 1000. *Cell voltage:* 12 V.
(Courtesy of *Analytical Chemistry*)

for the range 5.2×10^{-8} to 1.3×10^{-5} g ml^{-1} and in Fig. 4.8 for the range 1.3×10^{-5} to 1.3×10^{-3} g ml^{-1}. Four unknown samples were prepared by one analyst and analyzed by another with results tabulated in Table 4.3. Chloroform served as an internal standard in the preparation of the calibration curves and in the analysis of the unknowns.

A critical study of the application of gas chromatography to quantitative determination of metals in mixtures has been made by Schwarberg[53,54].

It was found that the trifluoroacetylacetonates of beryllium, aluminum, gallium and indium produced symmetrical, well-separated peaks which served for the determination of these

TABLE 4.3. APPLICATION OF METHOD TO UNKNOWN SAMPLES*

Cr(hfa)$_3$ concentration, g ml^{-1}		Deviation	
Actual	Found	Total, g ml^{-1}	%
4.0×10^{-6}	4.0×10^{-6}	—	—
2.1×10^{-6}	2.1×10^{-6}	—	—
2.0×10^{-7}	2.1×10^{-7}	0.1×10^{-7}	5.0
7.6×10^{-8}	8.6×10^{-8}	1.0×10^{-8}	13.2

* Courtesy of *Analytical Chemistry*.

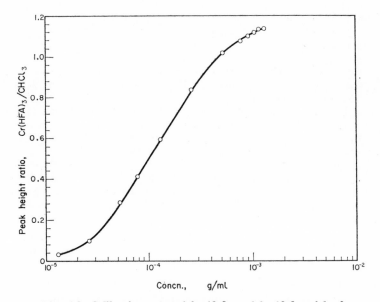

FIG. 4.8. Calibration curve 1.3×10^{-5} to 1.3×10^{-3} g ml^{-1} of Cr(hfa)$_3$. *Column:* 11 ft. *Temperature:* 90°. *Flash heater:* 170°. *Detector:* 200°. *Pressure:* 40 psig. *Split flow:* 300 ml min^{-1}. *Scavenge:* 200 ml min^{-1}. *Electrometer gain:* 300. *Cell voltage:* 17 V.
(Courtesy of *Analytical Chemistry*)

elements in synthetic mixtures with an overall relative mean error of ± 2 per cent. Thallium trifluoroacetylacetonate was included to find out if it would interfere when present in the mixture. It was found that the thallium complex was eluted prior to the other metal chelates without interference.

The work was performed on an F & M Model 500 gas chromatograph equipped with a thermal conductivity detector with W-2 filaments. A disc chart integrator on the recorder was used to determine peak areas. Samples were injected with a Hamilton 10 μl. syringe. A borosilicate glass insert in the injection port prevented any possible interaction of the injected sample with the metal of the port. The insert also served as a means of determining the presence of non-volatile matter in the sample and any thermal decomposition of the sample.

The columns were 4 ft × 4 mm i.d. borosilicate glass tubing in helical form. Three columns were used in the study. Column No. 1 was filled with 0.5 per cent by weight Dow Corning Silicone 710 oil coated on 60–80 mesh glass microbeads. Column No. 1s was similar to Column No. 1 except that both the tube and the microbeads were silanized by treatment with chlorotrimethylsilane, one volume per cent in carbon tetrachloride, at room temperature according to the procedure of Bohemen et al.,[55]. Column No. 2 was filled with 5.0 per cent by weight of Dow Corning Silicone 710 oil coated on 30–60 mesh Chromosorb W. Each column was conditioned before use by heating for 24 hr with a perceptible helium flow.

The metal trifluoroacetylacetonates were prepared from the purest metal or metal salt obtainable, using fractionated trifluoroacetylacetone (boiling point 106–7°C), by the procedure for the preparation of aluminum acetylacetonate[56]. They were purified by recrystallization from hexane, and then sublimed at 60–100°C/0.05 mm. The melting points agreed with literature values[57,58]. They were characterized by their infrared and ultraviolet spectra. The thallium compound was not completely characterized. Solutions of these chelates for gas chromatographic study were prepared in benzene in appropriate concentrations.

Results. The chelates were collected after elution and found to be identical to the injected material.

When Columns No. 1 and 2 were used, tailing of the chromatographic peaks was appreciable. When Column No. 1s was used tailing of all peaks was a minimum. A poor feature of Column No. 2 was the necessity for conditioning it by six injections of the gallium and indium chelates before reproducible peaks could be obtained.

In Fig. 4.4 is shown a chromatogram of all five metal chelates using Column No. 1. Temperature programming was used to sharpen the peaks and elute all five metal chelates in a reasonable time. Schwarberg recommended temperature programming in survey studies and in qualitative analyses and isothermal conditions for quantitative work.

For quantitative determinations Column No. 1s is recommended together with the following instrument conditions: isothermal column temperature; helium flow, 79 ml min^{-1}; injection port temperature, 135°C; block heater, 175°C.

Representative chromatograms are shown in Fig. 4.9, for thallium and beryllium, in Fig. 4.10 for beryllium, aluminum and

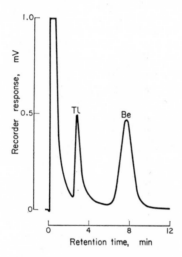

FIG. 4.9. The separation of the beryllium(II) trifluoroacetyl-acetonate from the thallium compound at a column temperature of 85°C.

gallium, and in Fig. 4.11 for aluminum, gallium and indium. The chromatograms were obtained using Column No. 1s. Overlapping peaks were obtained when Column No. 1 instead of Column No. 1s was used under the same instrument conditions.

A study was also made to determine if other metal trifluoro-acetylacetonates interfered with the determination of beryllium,

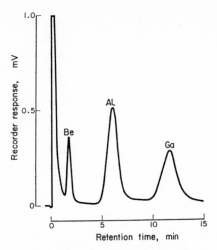

FIG. 4.10. The separation of the beryllium(II), aluminum(III) and gallium(III) trifluoroacetylacetonates using a column temperature of 115°C.

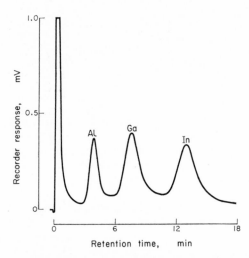

FIG. 4.11. Separation of the aluminum(III), gallium(III) and indium(III) trifluoroacetylacetonates at a column temperature of 120°C.

aluminum, gallium, and indium. In Table 4.4 is listed the order of elution obtained on Column No. 1 for several metal trifluoro-acetylacetonates. The retention times for some lie close to that of indium. If a change in instrument conditions cannot accomplish complete resolution of the indium peak from those of the impurities, then a preliminary chemical separation is in order. Partial decomposition or incomplete volatilization at an injection port temperature of 135°C is noticeable for the trifluoroacetylacetonates of iron(III), zinc, manganese(III), zirconium and hafnium (see Chapter 2). Further study is needed to determine whether or not this will interfere with the quantitative determination of other complexes.

TABLE 4.4. COMPARATIVE ORDER OF ELUTION
FOR VARIOUS METAL tfa's[a]

Metal tfa	Retention time (min)
Al	2.6
Ga(III)	4.8
Sc(III)	6.0
Cr(III)	7.5
Cu(II)	7.7
Mn(III)	8.2
In(III)	8.5
Zr	12.0
Hf	12.0
Zn	12.8
Th	[b]

[a] Column #1 at 125°C. Flow rate 83 ml min⁻¹.
[b] No peak up to 13 min.

In the quantitative study of the chelates of beryllium, aluminum, gallium, and indium, peak areas were reproducible to within 2 per cent under isothermal conditions. Whether alone or in mixtures each chelate produced identical chromatographic peaks with linearity in peak areas and in peak heights for solutions having concentrations of 2·5–10 weight/volume per cent. Rigid control of manipulative details is necessary, especially the length of time the needle is in the injection port.

9

A calibration curve was prepared for each of the four metal chelates. The points used were the mean values of 4–10 measurements and were reproducible within a relative mean error of two per cent. The average deviation when peak heights were used instead of peak areas was 2.4 per cent. The accuracy and precision were better when higher column temperatures were used. The minimum detectable limit for the beryllium trifluoroacetylacetonate was 0.04 μg of metal.

REFERENCES

1. G. H. MORRISON and H. FREISER, *Solvent Extraction in Analytical Chemistry*, Wiley, New York, 1957, pp. 157–247.
2. S. AHRLAND, *Acta Chem. Scand.*, **3**, 347 (1949).
3. J. BJERRUM, *Metal Ammine Formation in Aqueous Solution*, Dissertation, Copenhagen, 1941.
4. S. FRONAEUS, Dissertation, Lund, 1948.
5. N. H. FURMAN, W. B. MASON and S. PEKOLA, *Anal. Chem.*, **21**, 1325 (1949).
6. H. M. IRVING and R. J. WILLIAMS, *J. Chem. Soc.*, 1841 (1949).
7. I. M. KOLTHOFF and E. B. SANDELL, *J. Am. Chem. Soc.*, **63**, 1906 (1941).
8. I. LEDEN, *A. physik Chem.*, **A188**, 160 (1941).
9. A. E. MARTELL and M. CALVIN, *Chemistry of Metal Chelate Compounds*, Prentice-Hall, New York, 1952.
10. M. OOSTING, *Anal. Chim. Acta*, **21**, 301 (1959).
11. J. RYDBERG, *Acta Chem. Scand.*, **4**, 1503 (1950).
12. J. STARÝ and E. HLADKÝ, *Anal. Chim. Acta*, **28**, 227 (1963).
13. J. F. STEINBACH and H. FREISER, *Anal. Chem.*, **25**, 881 (1953).
14. J. F. STEINBACH and H. FREISER, *Anal. Chem.*, **26**, 375 (1954).
15. J. P. MCKAVENEY and H. FREISER, *Anal. Chem.*, **29**, 290 (1957).
16. E. ABRAHAMCZIK, *Mikrochemie ver. Mikrochim. Acta*, **33**, 208 (1947).
17. E. ABRAHAMCZIK, *Angew. Chem.*, **61**, 89, 96 (1949).
18. J. A. ADAM, E. BOOTH and J. D. H. STRICKLAND, *Anal. Chim. Acta*, **6**, 462 (1952).
19. A. W. KENNY, W. R. E. MATON and W. T. SPRAGG, *Nature*, **165**, 483 (1950).
20. A. G. MADDOCK and G. L. MILES, *J. Chem. Soc.*, S248 (1949).
21. T. Y. TORIBARA and P. S. CHEN, JR., *Anal. Chem.*, **24**, 539 (1952).
22. A. KRISHEN and H. FREISER, *Anal. Chem.*, **29**, 288 (1957).
23. R. A. BOLOMEY and A. BROIDO, U.S. Atomic Energy Comm. Report ORNL-196.
24. B. G. HARVEY, H. G. HEAL, A. G. MADDOCK and E. L. ROWLEY, *J. Chem. Soc.*, 1010 (1947).
25. R. PRIBIL and M. JELINEK, *Chem. listy*, **47**, 1326 (1953).
26. J. RYDBERG, *Arkiv Kemi*, **9**, 190 (1955); *Svensk Kem. Tidskr.*, **87**, 499 (1955).
27. J. RYDBERG, *Acta Chem. Scand.*, **4**, 1503 (1950).

28. H. W. CRANDALL and J. R. THOMAS, U.S.P. No. 2,892,681, June 30, 1959.
29. R. E. CONNICK and W. H. McVEY, *J. Am. Chem. Soc.*, **71**, 3182(1949).
30. E. H. HUFFMAN and L. J. BEAUFAIT, *J. Am. Chem. Soc.*, **71**, 3179(1949).
31. B. G. SCHULTZ and E. M. LARSEN, *J. Am. Chem. Soc.*, **72**, 3610(1950).
32. H. W. CRANDALL, J. R. THOMAS and J. C. REID, U.S. Atomic Energy Comm. CN-2657, 10 pp. (1945).
33. W. G. SCRIBNER, 148th National American Chemical Society Meeting, Chicago, Illinois, August 30–September 4, 1964.
33a. R. W. MOSHIER, Unpublished data.
34. J. E. HEVERAN, Masters Thesis, Purdue University, 1962.
35. W. W. BRANDT and J. E. HEVERAN, 142nd National Meeting, American Chemical Society, Atlantic City, New Jersey, Sept. 9–14, 1962.
36. W. D. ROSS and G. WHEELER, JR., *Anal. Chem.*, **36**, 266 (1964).
37. J. F. STEINBACH and J. H. BURNS, *J. Am. Chem. Soc.*, **80**, 1839 (1958).
38. B. G. SCHULTZ and E. M. LARSEN, *J. Am. Chem. Soc.*, **71**, 3250 (1949).
39. R. W. MOSHIER, J. E. SCHWARBERG, M. L. MORRIS and R. E. SIEVERS, Pittsburgh Conference on Analytical Chemistry and Applied Spectroscopy, Pittsburgh, Pa., March 5–9, 1963.
40. Columbia Organic Chemical Co., Columbia, South Carolina.
41. S. Y. TYREE, JR., *Inorganic Syntheses*, Vol. IV, McGraw-Hill, New York, 1953, pp. 104–11.
42. R. H. ATKINSON, J. STEIGMAN and C. F. HISKEY, *Anal. Chem.*, **24**, 477 (1952).
43. P. CAMBOULIVES, *Compt. rend.*, **150**, 175 (1910).
44. K. KNOX, S. Y. TYREE, JR., R. D. SRIVASTAVA, V. NORMAN, J. Y. BASSETT, JR. and J. H. HOLLOWAY, *J. Am. Chem. Soc.*, **79**, 3358 (1957).
45. A. B. BARDAWIL, F. N. COLLIER, JR. and S. Y. TYREE, JR., *Inorg. Chem.*, **3**, 149 (1964).
46. Scientific Kit Company, P.O. Box 244, Washington, Pennsylvania.
47. Instruments for Research and Industry, 108 Franklin Avenue, Cheltenham, Pennsylvania.
48. S. DAL NOGARE and R. S. JUVET, JR., *Gas–Liquid Chromatography, Theory and Practice*, Interscience, New York, 1962.
49. W. G. BALDWIN, Thesis, University of Manitoba, 1961.
50. R. D. HILL and H. GESSER, *J. Gas Chromatography*, **1**, 11 (Oct. 1963).
51. W. D. ROSS, *Anal. Chem.*, **35**, 1596 (1963).
52. D. K. ALBERT, *Anal. Chem.*, **36**, 2034 (1964).
53. J. E. SCHWARBERG, Masters thesis, University of Dayton, 1964.
54. J. E. SCHWARBERG, R. W. MOSHIER and J. H. WALSH, *Talanta*, **11**, 1213, 1964.
55. J. BOHEMEN, S. H. LANGER, R. H. PERRET and J. H. PURNELL, *J. Chem. Soc.*, 2444 (1960).
56. R. C. YOUNG, *Inorganic Syntheses*, Vol. II, W. C. Fernelius, ed., McGraw-Hill, New York, 1946, pp. 25.
57. R. C. FAY and T. S. PIPER, *J. Am. Chem. Soc.*, **85**, 500 (1963).
58. R. A. STANIFORTH, Doctoral Dissertation, Ohio State University, 1954.
59. W. D. ROSS, R. E. SIEVERS and G. WHEELER, JR., *Anal. Chem.*, **37**, 598 (1965).

CHAPTER 5

GAS CHROMATOGRAPHY IN
METAL COORDINATION CHEMISTRY

THE value of gas chromatography in studies of metal coordination compounds has not been widely recognized. This is not too surprising because its applicability to problems in this field has been demonstrated only very recently. Table 5.1 lists some of the applications of gas chromatography in coordination chemistry.

TABLE 5.1. SOME APPLICATIONS OF GAS CHROMATOGRAPHY
IN STUDIES OF METAL COMPLEXES

Subject	Investigators	Ref.
Resolution of $d-l$ isomers of Cr(hfa)$_3$	Sievers, Moshier, and Morris	11
Separation of cis–trans isomers of Cr(tfa)$_3$	Sievers, Ponder, Morris, and Moshier	12
Kinetics and equilibrium constants for the formation of mixed-ligand complexes in the Al(hfa)$_3$–Al(acac)$_3$ system.	Linck and Sievers	21
Kinetics of reaction of phenyl-magnesium bromide with 1-hexyne.	Guild, Hollingsworth, McDaniel, Podder and Wotiz.	22
Stoichiometry of tetrahydrofuran complexes of LiAlH$_4$, MgBr$_2$, R$_2$Mg and several Grignard reagents.	Guild, Hollingsworth, McDaniel, and Podder; Hollingsworth, Smalley, and Podder.	23, 24
Studies of metal–ligand interactions using metal complexes as column liquids.	Cartoni, Lowrie, Phillips and Venanzi.	26
Determination of stability constants of metal–olefin complexes.	Gil-Av and Herling.	32

124

Some of the techniques are applicable only to volatile metal complexes but others can be applied to the study of a great number of non-volatile complexes as well. In the coming years it seems certain that it will become an increasingly important technique in the hands of the metal coordination chemist.

RESOLUTION OF OPTICAL ISOMERS

The resolution of optical isomers of metal complexes has been accomplished by a variety of techniques[1]. These include: conversion to diastereoisomers; spontaneous crystallization of the antipodes and subsequent mechanical separation of the crystals; preferential crystallization by seeding with a crystal of one of the antipodes; and methods based on preferential adsorption of an optically active solid or differential solubility in an optically active liquid. The method involving the formation of diastereoisomers, with subsequent fractional crystallization, is the easiest and by far the most frequently employed. The resolution of uncharged inner complexes has always been exceptionally difficult because the technique of forming diastereoisomers cannot be used. In the few instances in which inner complexes have been resolved, the methods were based on differences in adsorption[2-7] or solubility in an asymmetric environment[8,9]. One form of the selective adsorption method is based on liquid–solid chromatography, in which a solution of the racemic mixture is passed through a column containing an optically active solid. The technique has been moderately successful, but it is likely that only partial separations have been accomplished[6].

Gas chromatography offers an intriguing approach to the separation of optical isomers. The direct resolution of optical isomers without the formation of diastereoisomers has far-reaching implications in several fields. But the task is formidable. Optical isomers have identical polarities and volatilities; therefore any differences in retentive properties can arise only from spatial considerations. The column must be able to exhibit stereospecificity, either in adsorption or solvation, and this can occur only if the column contains an optically active material.

In gas–solid chromatography resolution of isomers is based on differences in the adsorptive properties at the surface of the optically active solid. In resolution by gas–liquid chromatography, the stationary phase is an optically active liquid. The separation is based on stereospecificity of solvation, one isomer being solvated to a different extent than its mirror image. The existence of stereospecific solvation effects has been demonstrated by Patterson and Buchanan, who showed that, while the molecular volumes of a pair of enantiomers measured in a symmetrical solvent are identical, they differ in an asymmetric solvent[10]. On an asymmetric surface or in an asymmetric liquid, adsorption or solvation of one isomer may be thermodynamically or kinetically favored over that of the other isomer, thus establishing a basis for the separation.

The use of gas chromatography for the resolution of optical isomers of metal complexes was first reported by Sievers, Moshier and Morris[11]. The resolution was accomplished in a gas–solid system, using a column packed with powdered d-quartz. A sample of racemic dl-chromium(III) hexafluoroacetylacetonate (Fig. 5.1)

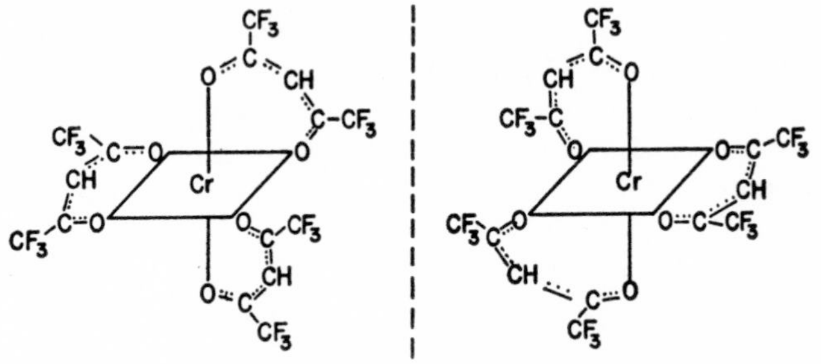

FIG. 5.1. Optical isomers of chromium(III) hexafluoroacetylacetonate[11].
(Courtesy of *Inorganic Chemistry*)

was passed through a 12 ft long column which was maintained at 55°C. Fractions were collected from the effluent helium stream and were checked for optical activity; an early fraction of the eluate was dextrorotary at the sodium D line, proving that at least a partial resolution was accomplished.

Gas–liquid chromatography has certain inherent advantages over gas–solid systems. Tailing is much less prevalent in gas–liquid systems; moreover, elution behavior is more reproducible. Attempts have been made to resolve several classes of compounds by gas–liquid chromatography*[12–14], but this approach has suffered from the paucity of suitable liquid stationary phases. A good liquid phase must meet the following criteria:

1. It must not racemize over reasonably long periods of time at the temperature at which the column is operated.

2. Its vapor pressure must be low enough that it does not bleed from the column in significant amounts at the operating temperature.

3. It must not solvate the optical isomers so strongly that column temperatures high enough to cause their racemization are required.

4. The optically active center must not be buried at such an unexposed position in the structure that stereospecificity in solvation will be precluded.

It should be emphasized that the appearance of two peaks in the chromatogram obtained when a racemic mixture is passed through an optically active column cannot be regarded as conclusive evidence that the mixture was resolved. It is necessary that fractions be collected and examined for optical activity before any positive conclusions can be drawn. Too many artifacts can give rise to double peaks to make their appearance acceptable evidence. For example, sample overloading, a poorly designed or insufficiently heated injection port, or an impurity in the sample can cause double peaks that could be mistakenly interpreted as arising from the separation of optical isomers.

SEPARATION OF GEOMETRICAL ISOMERS

The separation and simultaneous analysis of geometrical isomer mixtures is another potentially important application of gas chromatography in studies of stereochemistry. The technique is particularly effective for mixtures of isomers possessing only subtle differences in structure. The first application of this technique in

* For reviews of attempts to separate optical isomers of organic compounds by gas chromatography see references 13 and 14.

metal coordination chemistry was to the separation of the *cis* and *trans* isomers of chromium(III) trifluoroacetylacetonate[12]. If bidentate or multidentate ligands are unsymmetrical, the complexes formed from such ligands will usually exist in multiple isomeric forms. For example, the synthesis of octahedral complexes with unsymmetrical bidentate ligands yields two geometrically isomeric compounds[7,15–17]. The two isomers of the trifluoroacetyl-acetonato complexes are shown in Fig. 5.2. The structures are shown in simplified form so as to indicate more clearly the symmetry factors that give rise to the isomers. In the *cis* isomer all three trifluoromethyl groups are mutually adjacent and lie above the upper front face of the octahedron. One of the ligands is reversed in the *trans* isomer; therefore its trifluoromethyl group is still *cis* to one of the other CF_3 groups but *trans* to the remaining group. Because the CF_3 groups are all on the same side of the molecule in the *cis* compound, this isomer would be expected to be more polar than the *trans* compound.

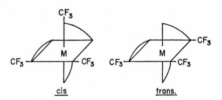

FIG. 5.2. Geometrical isomers of octahedral metal trifluoroacetylacetonates[12].
(Courtesy of *Inorganic Chemistry*)

The gas chromatographic separation of the *cis* and *trans* isomers of chromium(III) trifluoroacetylacetonate is shown in Fig. 5.3. As expected on the basis of the relative polarities of the isomers, the *trans* isomer was eluted prior to the *cis* isomer. The peak assignments were confirmed by collection and examination of eluate fractions. Recently the *cis* and *trans* isomers of rhodium(III) trifluoroacetylacetonate were separated by gas chromatography[18].

The gas chromatographic technique is most valuable when other methods for isomer analysis fail. The visible, ultraviolet, and infrared spectra of the two isomers of the chromium(III) complex are almost identical[16]; therefore, these spectroscopic techniques cannot be used for the determination of mixtures of the isomers without a prior separation step. Nuclear magnetic resonance spectroscopy also cannot be applied owing to the paramagnetism of the chromium(III) complex. The isomers can be separated by liquid–solid column chromatography[16] or by fractional crystallization from carbon tetrachloride[12], but both of these techniques

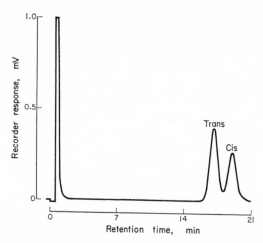

Fig. 5.3. Separation of *cis* and *trans* Cr(tfa)$_3$ by gas chromatography[12]. *Column:* copper tubing, 10 ft long, 0.25 in., o.d., packed with 5 per cent Dow Corning high-vacuum silicone grease on Chromosorb W (30–60 mesh). *Column temp.:* 115°C. *Helium flow rate:* 140 ml min^{-1}. *Sample:* 0.5 μl. of a 10 per cent solution of a mixture of the isomers in benzene.
(Courtesy of *Inorganic Chemistry*)

are unwieldy for such applications as the study of the kinetics of isomerization or the determination of isomer distributions during the course of ligand substitution reactions. The separation and analysis of the two-isomer component system is one of the simplest stereochemical problems to which gas chromatography is applicable. A more elegant application may be found in studies of mixed-ligand complexes in which the stereochemical possibilities are more complex. For example, in the hexafluoroacetylacetone–trifluoro-acetylacetone system there are seven chromium(III) complexes of the formula $Cr(tfa)_x(hfa)_{3-x}$. When $x = 3$, the two geometrical isomers described earlier are found. For $Cr(tfa)_2(hfa)$ there are three geometrical isomers, appearing as *cis–cis*, *cis–trans*, and *trans–cis* structures*. $Cr(tfa)(hfa)_2$ and $Cr(hfa)_3$ exist in single isomeric forms. Preliminary studies have indicated that the seven compounds can be separated by gas chromatography[19]. When mixtures of the chromium(III) complexes isolated from reaction mixtures of chromium(III) nitrate nonahydrate, trifluoroacetyl-acetone, and hexafluoroacetylacetone are passed through a column containing silicone grease liquid phase, the chromatogram shows seven peaks. The peak with the shortest retention time is $Cr(hfa)_3$. The next peak has been identified as $Cr(hfa)_2(tfa)$. The next three peaks have been tentatively assigned to the three isomers of $Cr(hfa)(tfa)_2$, while the sixth and seventh peaks have been identified definitely as *trans-* and *cis*-$Cr(tfa)_3$, respectively.

STUDIES OF KINETICS AND EQUILIBRIA

Possibly the most important and far-reaching applications of gas chromatography in metal coordination chemistry are in the areas of kinetics and equilibria. As will be seen in the following, some of the techniques are applicable to non-volatile complexes as well as volatile ones.

The case in which all of the reactants and products are volatile is particularly interesting because the concentrations of all the components can be followed as a function of time. This makes the technique valuable for following the kinetics of consecutive reactions, as well as studying simpler one-step reactions.

Dal Nogare and Juvet[20] have reviewed the use of gas chromatography in the measurement of reaction kinetics and equilibrium constants for several organic systems. Linck and Sievers[21] utilized gas chromatography to obtain rate data and equilibrium constants for the formation of mixed-ligand complexes in non-aqueous solvents. Mixtures of aluminum acetylacetonate and aluminum hexafluoroacetylacetonate undergo ligand exchange

---

* For a discussion of the nomenclature and a description of the structures see reference 17, which treats the analogous mixed-ligand complexes of acetylacetone and trifluoroacetylacetone.

reactions to form the mixed-ligand complexes, Al(hfa)₂(acac) and Al(hfa)(acac)₂. The system studied in most detail is shown in the following equation:

$$Al(acac)_3 + Al(hfa)_2(acac) \rightleftharpoons 2Al(hfa)(acac)_2.$$

All of the reactants and products were separated and analyzed by gas chromatography. As expected on the basis of the discussion in Chapter 2, the ease with which the complexes are eluted depends on the extent of fluorine substitution in the complexes. Al(hfa)₃ is eluted most readily, followed by Al(hfa)₂(acac), then Al(hfa)(acac)₂, and finally, Al(acac)₃ (see Fig. 5.4).

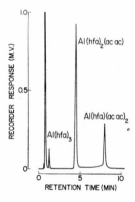

FIG. 5.4. Separation of mixed-ligand complexes of aluminum [21] *Column:* 4 ft × 4 mm i.d., packed with 5 per cent Dow-Corning High Vacuum Silicone Grease on Chromosorb W (30–60 mesh). *Column temp.:* programmed from 65 to 135°C at 7.9°C min⁻¹. *Injection port temp.:* 112°C. *Block temp.:* 168°C. *Helium flow rate:* 70 ml min⁻¹. *Sample:* 0.5μl. of a mixture of the complexes in CCl₄. *Detector signal attenuation:* × 8. *Instrument·* F & M Model 500. Under these conditions Al(acac)₃ has a much longer retention time than the other three complexes.

The method should also be applicable to the investigation of reactions in which one ligand is substituted for another, as in the following:

$$M(hfa)_3 + H(acac) \rightleftharpoons M(hfa)_2(acac) + H(hfa)$$
$$M(hfa)_2(acac) + H(acac) \rightleftharpoons M(hfa)(acac)_2 + H(hfa)$$
$$M(hfa)(acac)_2 + H(acac) \rightleftharpoons M(acac)_3 + H(hfa)$$

It is not necessary, of course, that all of the reactants and products be volatile. Even if only one of the components is volatile, gas chromatography can still be used to obtain kinetic data, although the data are necessarily more restricted in nature. Thus, the technique is applicable to countless reactions involving metal complexes with volatile ligands.

A variety of procedures can be employed to sample the volatile components; samples of the reaction mixture can be taken directly or after an intervening step designed to separate the component of interest from the reaction mixture. Guild *et al.*[22] used a clever method in which the sample is taken from the vapor in equilibrium with a refluxing reaction mixture. If one of the reactants is non-volatile, this technique affords a self-quenching method of sampling, thereby obviating possible problems arising from the accumulation of non-volatile reaction components in the injection port of the apparatus. The technique was used in studying the kinetics of the reaction of phenylmagnesium bromide with 1-hexyne in ethyl ether. The results were cross-checked by comparing the rate calculated for the appearance of benzene with that obtained for the disappearance of 1-hexyne.

Complex formation in mixed-solvents can be studied by measuring deviations in Henry's law behavior caused by metal–donor bond formation involving one of the solvents[23,24]. The partial pressures of volatile components in a multicomponent system are a measure of their respective activities. Complexation of a volatile component can be detected by examining the appropriate partial pressure–composition isotherms. In an illustrative case the metal complex is studied in a mixture of two volatile solvents, one of which may form a complex while the other is inert. The method uses the lowering of the vapor pressure of the co-solvent in the presence of a given amount of the solute to determine the extent of complex formation between the solute and co-solvent. The vapor pressure of the co-solvent is plotted as a function of the concentration of the co-solvent in the presence of a known amount of solute. When the curve shows a deviation from Henry's law, the amount of co-solvent that is bound to the solute can be estimated from the magnitude of the displacement as given by linear extrapolation. The intercept of the extrapolated linear portion of the curve with the axis corresponding to the concentration of the co-solvent gives an estimate of the value of x in the formula $M \cdot xL$, where M is the solute and L is the co-solvent. This technique has been used to determine the stoichiometry of tetrahydrofuran complexes of lithium aluminum hydride, magnesium bromide, dialkylmagnesium compounds and several Grignard reagents[23,24].

Let us consider next one of the most interesting but least exploited techniques, *viz.* the direct study of metal–ligand interactions within the chromatographic column. It has long been known that if the stationary phase in the column contains an appropriate metal ion, certain volatile solutes will be retained by the column much longer than would otherwise be expected. For example, solutes that are known to be good ligands are greatly retarded by columns containing metal salts or complexes. Molten stearates of manganese, cobalt, nickel, copper and zinc have been used as liquid phases and their behaviors toward various solutes relative to that of a hydrocarbon liquid phase have been examined[25]. In this study evidence was found for particularly strong interactions between various amines and the metal stearates. Cartoni, Lowrie, Phillips, and Venanzi[26] used the N-dodecylsalicylaldimines of nickel, palladium, platinum and copper, and the methyl-n-octylglyoximes of nickel, palladium and platinum as column liquids. They selected metal complexes that are coordinatively unsaturated, hoping thereby to detect evidence of complex formation in the vacant fifth and sixth coordination positions. The retention times of a large number of solutes were compared with those observed on conventional, totally organic liquid phases. They found that the metal complexes retard specifically those compounds that can function as ligands, particularly amines, alcohols, ketones and compounds containing double bonds. These investigators suggested that gas chromatography offers a particularly effective method of studying metal complex formation in instances when the interactions are weak or when the compounds are readily susceptible to hydrolysis. The retention data permit one to calculate equilibrium constants, free energies, heats and entropies for the reactions between the column liquids and a great variety of volatile ligands that may be passed through the column[27]. The measurements can be made over wide temperature ranges, affording a greater degree of flexibility than is ordinarily encountered in classical methods.

Phillips and Timms[27] suggested that it may be possible to study the kinetics of metal–ligand interactions within the column using the theory advanced by Klinkenberg[28]. They observed that sometimes the peaks caused by compounds that can function as ligands were very broad compared with those of non-ligand compounds. On a column containing a molten platinum complex, peaks caused by olefins not only appeared much later than those of paraffins of comparable volatility, but were greatly broadened as well. Sharp paraffin peaks superimposed on the very broad peaks arising from olefins with much lower molecular weights were observed in the chromatograms.

Olefins are also selectively retarded by liquid phases containing silver nitrate[29–32]. Gil-Av and Herling[32] have described the determination of stability constants of silver–olefin complexes by gas chromatography. If 1:1 stoichiometry is assumed for the silver–olefin complex, the relationship between the stability constant, $K = [Ag^+-olefin]/[olefin][Ag^+]$, and the partition coefficient (ratio of the concentrations of the solute in the stationary liquid phase and the gas phase) is given by $K = (k - k_0)/k_0 [Ag^+]$ where k is the partition coefficient of the olefin between the silver nitrate–glycol stationary phase and the gas phase, k_0 is the partition coefficient of the olefin between a sodium nitrate–glycol stationary phase and the gas phase, and $[Ag^+]$ is the silver ion concentration in moles per litre. The partition coefficients k and k_0 were calculated from the specific retention volumes of the olefin in the respective stationary liquids[32,33]. Stability constants for sixteen silver–olefin complexes were measured[32]. The data showed that steric as well as electronic factors affect the stability of the complexes. Methyl substituents at the double bond markedly reduce the stability; and, as the size of the substituent is increased, the stability is further decreased. To check the values obtained by gas chromatography, the stability constants for the complexes of cyclohexene and octene-1 were determined by an independent method[34,35]. The two methods gave values in good agreement, (cyclohexene 7.2 and octene 3.2, compared with 7.7 and 3.3, respectively, by gas chromatography).

OTHER APPLICATIONS

Gas chromatography is beginning to be recognized as an important tool in studies of the reactions of coordinated ligands. In studying the reaction of cyanopentabenzylisonitrileiron(II) with aliphatic aldehydes, Heldt[36] decomposed the complexes and separated and identified the reaction products by gas chromatography. Foster and Tobler[37] studied the thermal decomposition of organomercuric acetates by chromatography, identifying the products formed and measuring their product distribution. In natural product chemistry gas chromatography has been used to study the degradation products of porphyrins and chlorophyll derivatives[38,39]. Identification of the oxidation products provided valuable information concerning constitution of the chlorophyll derivatives. For other applications, particularly with simpler metal complexes, it may be more desirable to decompose the complexes by precipitation with H_2S or by hydrolysis rather than by oxidative degradation. By these routes the ligands will not be as likely to be drastically altered, and interpretation of the data will be easier.

Rund, Basolo and Pearson[40] used gas chromatography to determine the fate of ethanol in the alcohol-catalyzed formation of trans-$Rh(py)_4Cl_2^+$. The reaction was carried out in aqueous solution using equimolar amounts of $K_2[Rh(H_2O)Cl_5]$ and ethanol, and an excess of pyridine. When the reaction was over, the solution was acidified and the volatile material distilled. Chromatography of the distillate revealed that no perceptible amount of alcohol had disappeared and that only a trace of acetaldehyde had been formed. The data suggest that the acceleration of the reaction rate was due to catalysis rather than to stoichiometric reaction with the alcohol.

Ultrapurification of volatile metal compounds by preparative-scale gas chromatography is an application of potential practical importance[41,42]. Because gas chromatography is a highly efficient separation process, it is useful in purifying samples that contain impurities with very similar physical and chemical properties. The technique has been applied to the purification of π-cyclopentadienylmanganese tricarbonyl and chromium hexacarbonyl[42]. Only small samples can be effectively processed; however, and this proves to be a serious disadvantage. As more is learned about preparative-scale chromatography, perhaps this problem will be overcome.

REFERENCES

1. F. Basolo, *The Chemistry of the Coordination Compounds*, Ed. by J. C. Bailar, Jr., Reinhold, New York, 1956, p. 331, and references cited therein.
2. D. H. Busch and J. C. Bailar, Jr., *J. Am. Chem. Soc.*, **76**, 5352 (1954).
3. T. Moeller and E. Gulyas, *J. Inorg. Nuclear Chem.*, **5**, 245 (1958).
4. E. Ferroni and R. Cini, *J. Am. Chem. Soc.*, **82**, 2427 (1960).
5. T. S. Piper, *J. Am. Chem. Soc.*, **83**, 3908 (1961).
6. J. P. Collman, R. P. Blair, A. L. Slade and R. L. Marshall, *Chem. and Ind. (London)*, 141 (1962).
7. R. C. Fay and T. S. Piper, *Inorg. Chem.*, **3**, 348 (1964).
8. F. P. Dwyer and E. C. Gyarfas, *Nature*, **168**, 29 (1951).
9. V. F. Doron and S. Kirschner, *Inorg. Chem.*, **1**, 539 (1962).
10. T. S. Patterson and C. Buchanan, *J. Chem. Soc.*, 290 (1940).
11. R. E. Sievers, R. W. Moshier and M. L. Morris, *Inorg. Chem.*, **1**, 966 (1962).
12. R. E. Sievers, B. W. Ponder, M. L. Morris and R. W. Moshier, *Inorg. Chem.*, **2**, 693 (1963).
13. G. Goldberg and W. A. Ross, *Chem. Ind. (London)*, 657 (1962), and references cited therein.
14. G. Karagounis and E. Lemperle, *Z. Anal. Chem.*, **189**, 131 (1962).
15. R. C. Fay and T. S. Piper, *J. Am. Chem. Soc.*, **84**, 2303 (1962), and references cited therein.
16. R. C. Fay and T. S. Piper, *J. Am. Chem. Soc.*, **85**, 500 (1963).
17. R. A. Palmer, R. C. Fay and T. S. Piper, *Inorg. Chem.*, **3**, 875 (1964).
18. W. D. Ross, R. E. Sievers and G. Wheeler, Jr., *Anal. Chem.*, **37**, 598 (1965).
19. R. G. Linck, W. D. Ross, G. Wheeler, Jr. and R. E. Sievers, unpublished data.
20. S. Dal Nogare and R. S. Juvet, Jr., *Gas–Liquid Chromatography*, Interscience, New York, 1962.
21. R. G. Linck and R. E. Sievers, 148th National Meeting, American Chemical Society, Chicago, Ill., Sept. 1964.
22. L. V. Guild, C. A. Hollingsworth, D. H. McDaniel, S. K. Podder, and J. H. Wotiz, *J. Org. Chem.*, **27**, 762 (1962).
23. L. V. Guild, C. A. Hollingsworth, D. H. McDaniel and S. K. Podder, *Inorg. Chem.*, **1**, 921 (1962), and references cited therein.
24. C. A. Hollingsworth, E. W. Smalley and S. K. Podder, *Inorg. Chem.*, **3**, 222 (1964).
25. D. W. Barber, C. S. G. Phillips, G. F. Tusa and A. Berdin, *J. Chem. Soc.*, 18 (1959).
26. G. P. Cartoni, R. S. Lowrie, C. S. G. Phillips and L. M. Venanzi, *Gas Chromatography, 1960*, Ed. by R. P. W. Scott, Butterworths, London, p. 273.
27. C. S. G. Phillips and P. L. Timms, *Anal. Chem.*, **35**, 505 (1963).
28. A. Klinkenberg, *Chem. Eng. Sci.*, **15**, 255 (1961).
29. B. W. Bradford, D. Harvey and D. E. Chalkley, *J. Inst. Petrol.*, **41**, 80 (1955).
30. E. Gil-Av, J. Herling and J. Shabtai, *J. Chromatog.*, **1**, 508 (1958).

31. J. SHABTAI, J. HERLING and E. GIL-AV, *J. Chromatog.*, **2**, 406 (1959).
32. E. GIL-AV and J. HERLING, *J. Phys. Chem.*, **66**, 1208 (1962).
33. A. B. LITTLEWOOD, C. S. G. PHILLIPS and D. T. PRICE, *J. Chem. Soc.*, 1480 (1955).
34. S. WINSTEIN and H. J. LUCAS *J. Am. Chem. Soc.*, **60**, 836 (1938).
35. J. G. TRAYNHAM and J. K. OLECHOWSKY, *J. Am. Chem. Soc.*, **81**, 571 (1959).
36. W. Z. HELDT, *J. Org. Chem.*, **27**, 2608 (1962).
37. D. J. FOSTER and E. TOBLER, *J. Org. Chem.*, **27**, 834 (1962).
38. H. P. MORLEY, F. P. COOPER and A. S. HOLT, *Chem. and Ind.*, 1018 (1959).
39. D. W. HUGHES and A. S. HOLT, *Can. J. Chem.*, **40**, 171 (1962).
40. J. V. RUND, F. BASOLO and R. G. PEARSON, *Inorg. Chem.*, **3**, 658 (1964).
41. J. H. BOCHINSKI, K. W. GARDINER and R. S. JUVET, JR., *Ultrapurification of Semiconductor Materials*, Ed. by M. S. BROOKS and J. K. KENNEDY, Macmillan, New York, 1962, p. 239.
42. J. I. PETERSON, L. M. KINDLEY and H. E. PODALL, *Ultrapurification of Semiconductor Materials*, Ed. by M. S. BROOKS and J. K. KENNEDY, Macmillan, New York, 1962, p. 253.

METAL COMPOUNDS OF β-DIKETONES

METAL CHELATES OF 1,1,1-TRIFLUORO-2,4-PENTANEDIONE (tfa)

	References
Cu(II) blue–violet, m.p. 189°, sol. in ether, benzene, chloroform, carbon tetrachloride	[61, 113]
Be(II) white, m.p. 112°, sub. 104°	[131]
Mn(II) yellow crystalline	[44]
Al(III) cream-white, m.p. 117°, 121–2°, subl. 100° *trans* isomer	[44, 131]
Ga(III) white, m.p. 128.5–129.5°, *trans* isomer	[44]
In(III) ivory, m.p. 118–20° *trans* isomer	[44]
Cr(III) dark violet, *cis* isomer, m.p. 112–14°, *trans* isomer, m.p. 154.5–5.0°	[44]
Mn(III) dark green–brown, m.p. 113–4°, *trans* isomer	[44]
Fe(III) dark red, m.p. 114°, *trans* isomer	[44]
Co(III) green, *cis* isomer, m.p. 129–129.5°, *trans* isomer, m.p. 158–8.5°	[44]
Rh(III) yellow, *cis* isomer, m.p. 148.5–9.0°, *trans* isomer, m.p. 189.5–190°	[44]
Sc(III) white, m.p. 106–7°, subl. 90–95°	[131]
Y(III) white, m.p. 132°	[131]
La(III) m.p. 169°	[131]
Ce(III) yellow, m.p. 130–1°	[131]
Pr(III) yellow, m.p. 133–4°	[131]
Nd(III) pink, m.p. 133–4°	[131]
Sm(III) cream-white	[131]
Eu(III) white, m.p. 132–4°	[131]
Gd(III) white, m.p. 133–5°	[131]
U(IV) olive-green, m.p. 142–4°	[131]
Pu(IV)	[58]
Zr(IV) white crystals, m.p. 128–30°, subl. 115°/0.05 mm	[77a]
Hf(IV) white crystals, m.p. 125–128°, subl. 115°/0.05 mm	[77a]

METAL CHELATES OF 1,1,1,5,5,5-HEXAFLUORO-2,4-PENTANEDIONE (hfa)

	References
Cu(II) green monohydrate, m.p. 126–8°	[64c, 107]
Be(II) m.p. 70–1°	[64]
Zn(II) white, dihydrate, m.p. 153–4°	[107]
Mn(II) dihydrate, m.p. 155–6°	[107]
Fe(II) dihydrate, m.p. dec.	[107]
Co(II) dihydrate, m.p. 172–4°	[107]
Ni(II) dihydrate, m.p. 207–8°	[107]
Al(III) white, m.p. 73–4°	[64, 107]
Cr(III) green, m.p. 84–5°, subl. 25°	[64, 107]
Fe(III) red, m.p. 49°, subl. 35°	[107]
Rh(III), m.p. 114–5°	[107]
La(III) cream-white, m.p. 120–5°	[131]
Nd(III) pink, m.p. 117°, monohydrate, m.p. 115–21°	[107, 131]
Sm(III) cream-white, m.p. 125°	[131]
Zr(IV) m.p. 152–4°	[107]
Th(IV) m.p. 121–2°	[107]
U(IV) brown–green, m.p. 90°, subl. 70–80°/0.2 mm 40–50°/0.001 mm, b.p. 145° dec.	[59]

METAL CHELATES OF MISCELLANEOUS HALOGENATED β-DIKETONES

	References
Cu(II) of 3-chloro-2,4-pentanedione, green crystals, decomposes upon sublimation	[31, 64a]
Cu(II) of 1,1-dichloro-2,4-pentanedione, grey-green	[109]
Cu(II) of 3-bromo-2,4-pentanedione, green, decomposes upon sublimation	[64a, 129]
Cr(III) of 3-bromo-2,4-pentanedione, red-violet needles, sol. in CHCl₃	[128, 115]
Co(III) of 3-bromo-2,4-pentanedione, red-brown, m.p. 240–1°	[115]
Cr(III) of 1,3-dibromo-2,4-pentanedione, deep red crystals, soluble in ether, acetic acid, chloroform	[115]
Cu(II) of 1,3,5-tribromo-2,4-pentanedione, m.p. 149 to 52° dec.	[129]
Cu(II) of 3-iodo-2,4-pentanedione, green, m.p. 180° dec.	[64a, 129]
Cu(II) of 1,5-diiodo-2,4-pentanedione, green, m.p. 64–6°	[129]
Cu(II) of 3-bromo-1,5-diiodo-2,4-pentanedione, m.p. 64–8°	[52]

Cu(II) of 5,5,5-trifluoro-3-methyl-2,4-pentanedione,
green, m.p. 170, 4–171.9°   [113]
Cu(II) of 5,5,5-trifluoro-4-methyl-3,5-hexanedione, green,
m.p. 164–5°   [113]
Cu(II) of benzoyltrifluoroacetone, green, m.p. 243–4°   [113]
Cu(II) of *p*-xenyltrifluoroacetone, green, m.p. 303°   [113]
Cu(II) of *p*-fluorobenzoyltrifluoroacetone, green, m.p.
263–4°   [113]
Cu(II) of 2-naphthoyltrifluoroacetone, green, m.p. 278.5 to
9.5°   [89]
Cu(II) of 2-thenoyltrifluoroacetone, green, m.p. 242–3°,
decomposes upon sublimation   [64a, 89, 64c]
Cu(II) of 2-furoyltrifluoroacetone, decomposes upon
sublimation   [64a, 64c]
Cu(II) of 2-thenoylperfluorobutyrylmethane, green,
decomposes upon sublimation   [64a]

1,1,1,2,2,3,3,7,7,7-*Decafluoro*-4,6-*heptanedione*
Cu(II) m.p. 73–83°, subl. 50°/0.1 mm   [153]
Ca(II) subl. 100°/0.005 mm   [153]
Sr(II) m.p. 170–186°   [153]
Ba(II) m.p. 145–180° dec.   [153]
Mg(II) m.p. 175–192°, subl. 135°/0.005 mm   [153]
Zr(IV) liquid, distilled 65–70°/0.005 mm   [153]
Hf(IV) liquid, distilled 70°/0.02 mm   [153]

1,1,1,2,2,6,6,6-*Octafluoro*-3,5-*hexanedione*
Cu(II) vivid green crystals, m.p. 76–79°, subl. at 25°/0.005 mm   [153]
Cr(III) liquid, distilled at 25°/0.001 mm   [153]

4,4,4-*Trifluoro*-1-*phenyl*-1,3-*butanedione*
Cu(II) crystals, m.p. 237.5–238.5°   [113, 153]

METAL CHELATES OF
2,4-PENTANEDIONE (acac)

References

Li yellow, dec., on heating, sol. water, hot
ethanol   [102, 152]
Na unstable with H_2O, chars on heating, sol. ethanol
217–9°   [24, 25, 60, 102]
Kunstable with H_2O, chars on heating, sol. ethanol, m.p.
261–3°   [60, 102]
Cs unstable with H_2O, chars on heating; sol. water, ethanol   [102]

Cu(I) rose-red, sol. methanol   [41, 144]
Ag decomposes spontaneously at room temperature   [89, 102]
Tl(I) monocl. needles, m.p. 153°, 160°, 168° (dec.) sol.   [45, 60, 75,
    water, ethanol   84, 102, 141, 142]
Se(I) Se₂(acac)₂   [9, 22, 68]
Cu(II) blue,
    m.p. 236° dec; subl.   [9, 19, 20, 22, 25, 64b, 64c, 28, 31, 68, 80]
Be(II) white, m.p. 108.1–108.6°, b.p. 270° subl. 90°/0.02 mm,
    soluble in hexane, benzene, cyclohexane   [3, 6, 12, 25, 26, 28, 47,
                                                   56, 60, 102, 110, 111]
Mg(II) white, prisms, m.p. 265–7°, sol. in hexane, benzene,
    cyclohexane   [25, 50, 60, 135]
Zn(II) white needles, anhydrous, m.p. 124, 137, 138°, subl.
    350°mm, sol. in ethanol, benzene; hydrolyzes in hot
    water   [50, 55, 56, 102, 120, 135]
Zn(II) monohydrate   [154]
Cd(II) white, needles, anhydrous, m.p. 177, 187°, subl.   [102, 120, 135]
Hg(II) white, m.p. 70° (dec.)   [55, 82, 102, 135]
Ca(II) tablets, dihydrate   [50, 102, 135]
Sr(II) dihydrate, slt. sol. ethanol   [50, 102, 153]
Ba(II) tablets, dihydrate   [102, 153]
Pb(II) hydrolyzes, sol. ethanol   [25, 28, 85]
Mn(II) yellow dihydrate, dehydrates at 50° (*vacuo*), subl.
    200°/2 mm, readily oxidized, tan, anhydrous, 250° dec.,
    sol. pyridine   [6, 18, 41, 144]
MoO₂(II) yellow, tablets, m.p. 175° dec. at 230°, subl.
    90° sol. in benzene, ethanol, chloroform   [55, 92]
Fe(II) brown–red, 1½ hydrate, dehydrates at 80°/*vacuo*, sol.
    in toluene, subl. 145–150°   [25, 28, 39, 40, 55, 144]
Ni(II) green, m.p. 230°   [6, 17a, 18a, 25, 28, 29a, 42a, 55, 80,
                                                                90, 144]
Co(II) pink, hydrate, dehydrates readily, sublimes, sol. in
    warm water and in chloroform   [5, 25, 28, 55, 80, 97, 102, 120, 144]
Pt(II) yellow, also bis(acetylacetonato)platinum(II). 2KCl   [122, 144]
Au(III) bis(methyl)acetylacetonato gold(III) m.p. 84°   [14]
bis(ethyl)acetylacetonato gold(III) m.p. 110°   [53]
B(III) chloro-bis(acetylacetonato)boron(III)   [14, 53, 59]
B(III) difluoro-diboron acetylacetonate, m.p. 43°   [106]
B(III) bis(acetylacetonato)boron(III) acetate, triiodide, etc.   [34]
Al(III) white, monoclinic prisms, m.p. 198° corr., b.p.
    314.0–316.6°, sol. benzene, subl. 100°/1 mm, 140°/10 mm
        [4, 7, 24, 26, 27, 55, 57, 60, 67, 68, 74, 77, 118, 128, 134, 140, 146]
Ga(III) white, monoclinic, sublimes 140/10 mm, sol.
    chloroform, benzene   [8, 67]
In(III) rhombic bipyrimidal   [9, 67, 93, 112, 115, 116]

Sc(III) white, rhombic bipyramidal, m.p. 187.0–187.5°,
188°, soluble in ethanol, ether, chloroform, benzene,
subl. 157°/8 mm, 360° dec.   [11, 34, 16, 68, 78, 88, 93, 102]
Y(III) needles, m.p. 114, 131°, b.p. dec.   [80, 102, 132, 138]
La(III) crystalline hydrate, m.p. 151, 142, 185°   [70, 83, 102, 132, 138]
Ce(III) yellow hydrate, m.p. 145, 165°   [7, 132]
Pr(III) m.p. 143, 146°; also a 2½ hydrate   [42, 65]
Nd(III) pink, m.p. 144, 150–2°, b.p. dec.   [7, 32, 70, 83]
Sm(III) m.p. 144, 146–7°; b.p. dec.; sol. ethanol, carbon
disulfide   [42, 132]
Eu(III) white, 3 hydrate, m.p. 136–7°, 144°, sol. ethanol,
benzene, chloroform, carbon tetrachloride   [127, 132]

Gd(III) white, monohydrate, m.p. 140°, no sublimate,
sol. ethanol, chloroform   [51, 70, 83, 127, 138]
Dy(III)   [83]
Tm(III) crystalline monohydrate, does not sublime   [71]
Yb(III), m.p. 114°   [83]
V(III) dark brown tablets and prisms, m.p. 185–90°, sol.
ether, acetone, chloroform, benzene   [101, 121]
Cr(III) red–violet monoclinic prisms, m.p. 214, 216°, b.p.
340°, subl. 100°/*vacuo*   [4, 46, 47, 55, 140]
Po(III)   [130]
Mn(III) black or dark brown monoclinic prisms, m.p. 172°;
dec. above 150°; soluble in methanol   [17, 37, 40, 55, 140]
Fe(III)red–brown rhombic pyramidal, m.p. 181.3° $[D]_4^{25}$
1.33, soluble ethanol, chloroform, benzene   [4, 12, 25, 28, 41, 47,
55, 57, 63, 77, 102, 114, 140, 144]
Co(III) dark green monoclinic prisms, m.p. 240–1°   [4, 15, 25, 28, 47,
55, 102]
Ni(III)   [25, 28, 55]
Rh(III) orange–yellow, m.p. 260°, dec. at 280° subl.
240/1.0 mm   [38a]
Ir(III) yellow, m.p. 269°, dec. 290°, subl. 260/1.0 mm   [38a]
Si(IV) tris(acetylacetonato)silicon(IV) acetate   [96, 116]
Si(IV) tris(acetylacetonato)silicon chloride, hydrochloride,
dec. at 171–4°   [34, 117, 122, 145]
Si(IV) tris(acetylacetonato)silicon tetrachloroferrate(III),
m.p. 184–6°   [34, 116, 117]
Si(IV) tris(acetylacetonato)silicon trichlorozincate, dec.
above 190°   [34, 96, 116, 117, 145]
Ti(IV) yellow, m.p. 146–7°   [34, 122]
Ti(IV) tris(acetylacetonato)titanium acetate, sol. acetic
acid   [34]

Ti(IV)   dichlorobis(acetylacetonato)titanium(IV),   red–orange crystalline, dec. at 230°   [34, 36, 141, 150]

Ti(IV)   bis[tris(acetylacetonato)titanium(IV)] hexachloro-platinate(IV), brownish-yellow prisms   [34]

Ti(IV)   tris(acetylacetonato)titanium(IV)   tetrachlorofer-rate(III), red–yellow, sol. benzene, chloroform

[7, 10, 34, 36, 65, 122, 150, 155]

Hf(IV) monoclinic decahydrate, anhydrous 193–5° dec., subl. 82°/0.001 mm $[D]_4^{25}$ 1.670, sol. in ethylene bromide   [10, 34, 62]

Zr(IV) white, monoclinic, forms decahydrate, anhydride, m.p. 194–5°, subl. 120°/1 mm; $[D]_4^{25}$ 1.415, sol. in ethylene bromide, carbon disulfide, carbon tetrachloride   [10, 91, 147]

Zr(IV)   tris(acetylacetonato)zirconium(IV)   chloride, prisms, m.p. 101–2°   [91]

Zr(IV) bis(acetylacetonato)zirconium(IV) chloride   [69]

Th(IV) m.p. 170.8–171.0, 171.5, 176.8°, b.p. 260–70° dec., subl. 160°/8 mm   [10, 62, 102, 108, 137, 148, 149]

Ge(IV)   bis(acetylacetonato)germanium(IV)   chloride, prisms, m.p. 240° dec., soluble in benzene and chloro-form   [96]

Ge(IV) bis(acetylacetonato)germanium(IV) bromide, m.p. 128–9°   [34, 93]

Ge(IV)   tris(acetylacetonato)germanium(IV)   dichloro copper(II)   [96]

Sn(IV) yellow, m.p. 146–7°   [7, 10, 34, 122, 134]

Sn(IV) bis(acetylacetonato)tin(IV) chloride, m.p. 202–3° dec.

Sn(IV) bis(acetylacetonato)tin(IV) bromide, prisms, m.p. 187°

Pa(IV)   [81]

Po(IV)   [130]

Ce(IV) dark red needles, undecahydrate, m.p. 174°, anhydride, m.p. 165°, 171–2° sol. chloroform   [72, 137]

V(IV) vanadyl bis(acetylacetonate), blue–green prisms, m.p. dec., sol. in ethanol, chloroform   [8, 101, 123, 126, 136]

U(IV) yellow–green, m.p. 176–7° dec., sol. in ether, toluene   [9, 10, 49, 59]

Pt(IV) orange–yellow   [144]

Pt(IV) bis(acetylacetonato) platinum(IV) chloride, potas-sium chloride

Pt(IV) bis(acetylacetonato) platinum(IV) chloride, disodium chloride

Pu(IV)   [58]

Sb(V) acetylacetonatoantimony(V) tetrachloride pris-
matic needles, m.p. 127, 137° [34, 122]
Nb(V) dichloro-oxyacetylacetonatoniobium(V), decom-
poses above 200°, insoluble in all solvents [35]
Nb(V) $K_2HNbO(acac)_3 \cdot 1.5H_2O$ [52, 125]
Nb(V) $Nb(OCH_3)_2Cl_2(acac)$ yellow plates, m.p. 128°
Nb(V) $Nb(OCH_2CH_3)_2Cl_2(acac)$ yellow plates, m.p. 74°
Ta(V) $Ta(OCH_3)_2Cl_2(acac)$ yellow prisms, m.p. 113° [52, 125]
Ta(V) $Ta(OCH_2CH_3)_2Cl_2(acac)$ yellow prisms, m.p. 63°
Mo(V) red–orange $Mo(OH)_3(acac)_2 \cdot 3H_2O$ hydrolyzes, sol.
benzene [124]
Mo(V) green $MoO_2(acac)$ hygroscopic, 150° dec. [92]
Mo(VI) yellow crystals, $MoO_2(acac)_2$ [92, 119]
Al(III) diethoxy(acetylacetonato)Al(III), b.p. 188°/4 mm,
yellow liquid [83a]
Al(III) diisopropoxy(acetylacetonato)Al(III), b.p. 160°/5
mm, yellow solid [83a]
Al(III) ethoxy bis(acetylacetonato)Al(III), yellow crystals [83a]
Al(III) isopropoxy bis(acetylacetonato)Al(III), yellow
crystals [83a]
Al(III) diethoxy(benzoylacetonato)Al(III), yellow crystals [83a]
Al(III) diisopropoxy(benzoylacetonato)Al(III), yellow
crystals [83a]
Al(III) ethoxy bis(benzoylacetonato)Al(III), yellow crystals [83a]
Al(III) isopropoxy bis(benzoylacetonato)Al(III), yellow
crystals [83a]
Al(III) ethylacetoacetate bis(acetylacetonato)Al(III), yellow
powder [83a]

METAL COMPOUNDS OF MISCELLANEOUS β-DIKETONES

3-*Methyl*-2,4-*pentanedione*
Cu(II) [64b, 64c]
VO(II) green prisms, m.p. dec., sol. in benzene, chloro-
form [101]

2,4-*Hexanedione*
Cu(II) blue needles, m.p. 197–8°, sol. in ethanol [54]
Be(II) crystals, m.p. 52.5–53.5°, sol. in ligroin [133]
GeCl₂(II) crystals, m.p. 128–9° [96]
Se₂(II), m.p. 137 [104]
Fe(III) red prisms, m.p. 45° (crystallizes with 2 moles
chloroform) [76]

MoO$_2$(II) brown crystals from ethanol, m.p. 185°; green
crystals from chloroform, m.p. 130°, sol. in ethanol,
acetone, chloroform, benzene [92]

3-*Methyl-2,4-pentanedione*
Ti(IV) as Ti(β-diketone)$_3$acetate; forms double salts with
metal chlorides [34]
Si(IV) as Si(β-diketone)$_3$acetate; forms double salts with
metal chlorides [34]
TeCl$_2$(II) yellow crystals, decomposed by water [94, 96]

3-*Ethyl-2,4-pentanedione*
Cu(II) m.p. 210–12°, sol. in ethanol, chloroform [64b, 64c, 32]
Se(II) [97]
TeCl$_2$(I) [94, 103]

2,4-*Heptanedione*
Cu(II) light blue crystals, m.p. 161, 164–5°, sol. in
ethanol, ether [13, 22, 64b, 64c, 95]

3,5-*Heptanedione*
Tl(I) needles, m.p. 70° [87]
Cu(II) blue needles, m.p. 206, 209–210°, sol. in ethanol,
benzene [48, 152]
Be(II) m.p. 63°, sol. in benzene [86]
Al(III) crystals from chloroform as Al(β-diketone)$_3$ · 2chlo-
roform sol. in chloroform [76, 95]
MoO$_2$(II) brown tablets, m.p. 78°, sol. in ethanol, acetone,
chloroform, benzene [92]

2-*Methyl-3,5-hexanedione*
Cu(II) blue needles, m.p. 171° [29]

3-*Methyl-2,4-hexanedione*
Cu(II) blue or green–gray needles, m.p. 195, 175–7° dec.,
respectively [20, 95]

2,4-*Octanedione*
Cu(II) m.p. 194° [99]

3,5-*Octanedione*
Cu(II) bright blue crystals, m.p. 158.5°, sol. in ethanol [38]

2-*Methyl-4,6-heptanedione*
Tl(I) needles, m.p. 70°, sol. in 50 per cent glycerol [87]
Cu(II) blue crystals, m.p. 195°, sol. in ether [13]

2-Methyl-5,7-heptanedione
Cu(II) m.p. 120°   [30]

3-Methyl-2,4-heptanedione
Cu(II) green–gray needles, m.p. 163°, sol. in ethanol,
  chloroform   [13]

4-Methyl-3,5-heptanedione
Cu(II) m.p. 172–4·, subl.   [66]

2-Methyl-4,6-heptanedione
Cu(II), m.p. 154°   [95]

6-Methyl-2,4-heptanedione
Cu(II) subl. 110°/0.005 mm, sol. in chloroform   [64a]

3-Ethyl-4,6-hexanedione
Cu(II) blue-black crystals, m.p. 68°, sol. in ether   [30]

2,2-Dimethyl-3,5-hexanedione
Cu(II) dark blue needles, m.p. 175, 190, 191–5°, subl.
  sol. in ligroin   [1, 30, 73, 94]

4,6-Nonanedione
Cu(II) blue, m.p. 158°, b.p. dec., sol. in ethanol   [1, 79, 105]

2,4-Nonanedione
Cu(II) blue crystals, m.p. 136°, sol. in organic solvents   [13]

2,2-Dimethyl-3,5-heptanedione
Ni(II) green at 0°, red at 50°   [42a]

2-Methyl-3,5-octanedione
Cu(II) blue needles, m.p. 123°   [13]

2-Methyl-6,8-octanedione
Cu(II) blue crystals, m.p. 112°, sol. in ether   [30]

2-Methyl-5,7-octanedione
Cu(II) blue crystals, m.p. 114°   [2]

3-Ethyl-2,4-heptanedione
Cu(II) silver-gray needles, m.p. 165° dec., sol. in benzene   [95, 98]

2,6-*Dimethyl*-3,5-*heptanedione*
Cu(II) m.p., 125–7°   [29a, 56a]
Ni(II) blue dihydrate, green anhydride, m.p. 155°, subl.
   150°; sol, in dichloroethane   [18a, 29a]

2,4-*Decanedione*
Cu(II) blue crystals, m.p. 122°   [22]

2-*Methyl*-4,6-*nonanedione*
Cu(II) blue crystals, m.p. 136–7°, sol. in methanol   [1]

3-*Methyl*-4,6-*nonanedione*
Cu(II) gray crystals, m.p. 122–4°   [1]

2,2,6,6-*Tetramethyl*-3,5-*heptanedione*
Ni(II) red, m.p., 217–221°, sol. in dichloroethane   [42a, 56b]

2,4-*Tridecanedione*
Cu(II) m.p. 113–4°   [99]

6,8-*Tridecanedione*
Cu(II) blue crystals, m.p. 119–20°   [99]

2,4-*Pentadecanedione*
Cu(II) m.p. 116.5–117.0°   [99]

2,2,4-*Trimethyl*-4-*tert-butyl*-5,7-*octanedione*
Cu(II) m.p. 166–8°   [99]

2,4-*Heptadecanedione*
Cu(II) blue–gray crystals, m.p. 117–9°   [99]

3,3,7,7-*Tetraethyl*-4,6-*nonanedione*
Cu(II) purple–red crystals, m.p. 143–4°   [143]

1-*Phenyl*-1,3-*butanedione*
Cu(II)   [64b, 64c]
Al(III) white, *trans* m.p. 223.5–4.0°   [43]
Cr(III) dark red *cis* m.p. 199.5°, *trans* m.p. 235°, γ-cis
   m.p. 196–196.5°   [43]
Mn(III) black, *trans* m.p. 173–173.5°   [43]
Co(III) green, *cis* m.p. 158–9°, *trans* m.p. 199.5–200°   [43]
Rh(III) yellow–orange, *cis* m.p. 218°, *trans* m.p. 260.5 to
   261.5°   [43]
Fe(III) red, *trans* m.p. 210–11°   [43]

Be(II) m.p. 155°   [91]
ZrO(II)   [91]

Dibenzoylmethane
Be(II) m.p. 191°   [12a, 106]

1,3-*Diphenyl-1,3-propanedione*
Cu(II)   [64b, 64c]

3-*Phenyl*-2,4-*pentanedione*
Cu(II)   [64c]

3-*Benzyl*-2,4-*pentanedione*
Cu(II)   [64c]

Dipivaloylmethane
Li(I) white powder, m.p. dec., subl.   [56b]
Na(I) white powder, m.p. dec., subl.   [56b]
K(I) white powder, m.p. dec., subl.   [56b]
Be(II) white needles from methanol, m.p. 93–7°   [56b]
Mg(II) white needles from petroleum ether, m.p. 94°
  (134°?)   [56b]
Ca(II) white needles from ethanol, m.p. 224°   [56b]
Sr(II) white needles from ethanol, m.p. 200°   [56b]
Ba(II) white needles from ethanol, m.p. 172°   [56b]
Co(II) purple or ruby-red crystals, monomeric, m.p. 143°,
  sublimes 110°/vacuo, sol. in petroleum ether, cyclo-
  hexane, benzene   [29b, 56b]
Ni(II) pink needles, m.p. 225°, subl.   [42a 56b]
Cu(II) deep blue prisms from n-heptane, m.p. 198°   [56b]
Zn(II) white needles, m.p. 144°, subl.   [56b]
Hg(II) white needles from methanol, m.p. 225°, a second
  compound, m.p. 192°, sublimes   [56b]
Al(III) white needles from ethanol, m.p. 264–5°   [56b]
Cr(III) purple crystals, m.p. 229°, subl.   [56b]
Mn(III) black crystals, m.p. 165°, subl.   [56b]
Fe(III) red needles from dimethylformamide, m.p. 163°,
  subl.   [56b]
Co(III) dark green crystals, m.p. 245°, subl.   [56b]
La(III) white needles from dimethylformamide, m.p.
  148–9°   [56b]
Sm(III) white needles from dimethylformamide, m.p.
  143–4°   [56b]
Ho(III) white needles from dimethylformamide, m.p.
  154–5°   [56b]

Er(III) pink needles from dimethylformamide, m.p.
153-4° [56b]

Benzoylpivaloylmethane
Li(I) white powder from acetone, m.p. dec. [56b]
K(I) white needles from acetone, m.p. dec. [56b]
Ca(II) white needles from methanol, m.p. dec. [56b]
Ba(II) white needles from ethanol, m.p. dec. [56b]
Cu(II) gray–green needles from petroleum ether, m.p. 202° [56b]
Ni(II) crystals from petroleum ether, m.p. 243° [56b]

REFERENCES

1. J. T. ADAMS and C. R. HAUSER, *J. Am. Chem. Soc.*, **66**, 1220 (1944).
2. E. ANDRÉ, *Ann. Chim.*, (8) **29**, 540 (1913).
3. A. ARCH and R. C. YOUNG, *Inorganic Syntheses*, Vol. II, McGraw-Hill, New York, 1946, p. 17.
4. W. T. ASTBURY, *Proc. Roy. Soc.*, **A112**, 449 (1926).
5. R. H. BAILES and M. CALVIN, *J. Am. Chem. Soc.*, **69**, 1892 (1947).
6. E. W. BERG and J. T. TRUEMPER, *J. Phys. Chem.*, **64**, 487 (1960).
7. W. BILTZ, *Ann.*, **331**, 334 (1904).
8. W. BILTZ, *Z. anorg. Chem.*, **40**, 219 (1904).
9. W. BILTZ, *Z. anorg. Chem.*, **82**, 438 (1913).
10. W. BILTZ and J. A. CLINCH, *Z. anorg. Chem.*, **40**, 219 (1904).
11. H. BOMMER, *Z. anorg. Chem.*, **248**, 397 (1941).
12. H. S. BOOTH and G. G. TORREY, *J. Phys. Chem.*, **35**, 2471 (1931).
12a. H. S. BOOTH and D. G. PIERCE, *J. Phys. Chem.*, **37**, 59 (1933).
13. L. BOUVEAULT and A. BONGERT, *Compt. rend.*, **132**, 703 (1901); *Bull. Soc. Chim.*, (3) **27**, 1084 (1902).
14. F. H. BRAIN and C. S. GIBSON, *J. Chem. Soc.*, 762 (1939).
15. B. E. BRYANT and W. C. FERNELIUS, *Inorganic Syntheses*, Vol. V, McGraw-Hill, New York, 1957, p. 188.
16. C. CHABRIE and E. RENGADE, *Compt. rend.*, **131**, 1300 (1900).
17. R. G. CHARLES and B. E. BRYANT, *Inorganic Syntheses*, Vol. VII, McGraw-Hill, New York, 1963, pp. 183, 184.
17a. G. J. BULLEN, *Nature*, **177**, 537 (1956).
18. R. G. CHARLES, *Inorganic Syntheses*, Vol. VI, McGraw-Hill, New York, 1960, p. 164.
18a. R. G. CHARLES and M. A. PAWLIKOWSKI, *J. Phys. Chem.* **62**, 440 (1958).
19. B. CIOCCA, *Gazz. Chim. Ital.*, **67**, 346 (1937).
20. L. CLAISEN, *Ann.*, **277**, 162 (1893).
21. L. CLAISEN and N. STYLOS, *Ber.*, **21**, 1144 (1888).
22. L. CLAISEN and E. F. EHRHARDT, *Ber.*, **22**, 1010 (1889).
23. J. P. COLLMAN, *Inorganic Syntheses*, Vol. VII, McGraw-Hill, New York, 1963, p. 134.
24. A. COMBES, *Ann. Chim.*, (6) **12**, 199 (1887).

25. A. COMBES, *Compt. rend.*, **105**, 869 (1887).
26. A. COMBES, *Compt. rend.*, **108**, 415 (1889).
27. A. COMBES, *Bull. Soc. Chim.*, (3) **1**, 345.
28. A. COMBES, *Compt. rend.*, **119**, 1222 (1894).
29. M. CONRAD and R. GAST, *Ber.*, **31**, 1342 (1898).
29a. F. A. COTTON and J. P. FACKLER, JR., *J. Am. Chem. Soc.*, **83**, 2818 (1961).
29b. F. A. COTTON and R. H. SODERBERG, *Inorg. Chem.*, **3**, 1 (1964).
30. F. COUTURIER and G. VIGNON, *Compt. rend.*, **140**, 1696 (1905).
31. E. G. COX and K. C. WEBSTER, *J. Chem. Soc.*, 733 (1935).
32. R. S. CURTISS, *Am. Chem. J.*, **17**, 436 (1895).
33. C. E. DENOON, JR., *Organic Syntheses*, **20**, 6 (1940).
34. W. DILTHEY, *Ann.* **344**, 300–342; *Ber.*, **36**, 923 (1903); *Ber.*, **37**, 589 (1904).
35. C. DJORDJEVIĆ and V. KATOVIĆ, *Chem. and Ind.*, 411 (1963).
36. V. DORON, *Inorganic Syntheses*, Vol. VII, McGraw-Hill, New York, 1963, p. 50.
37. U. DREHMANN, *Z. Physik Chem.*, **B53**, 228 (1943).
38. G. DUPONT, *Compt. rend.*, **148**, 1523 (1909).
38a. F. P. DWYER and A. M. SARGESON, *J. Am. Chem. Soc.*, **75**, 984 (1953).
39. B. EMMERT and B. JARCZYNSKI, *Ber.*, **64**, 1072 (1931).
40. B. EMMERT and H. GSOTTSCHNEIDER, *Ber.*, **66**, 1871 (1933).
41. B. EMMERT, H. GSOTTSCHNEIDER and H. STANGER, *Ber.*, **69**, 1321 (1936).
41a. B. EMMERT and E. JACOB, *Ber.*, **67B**, 289 (1934).
42. F. EPHRAIM and P. RAY, *Ber.*, **62**, 1519 (1929).
42a. J. P. FACKLER, JR. and F. A. COTTON, *J. Am. Chem. Soc.*, **82**, 5005 (1960).
43. R. C. FAY and T. S. PIPER, *J. Am. Chem. Soc.*, **84**, 2303 (1962).
44. R. C. FAY and T. S. PIPER, *J. Am. Chem. Soc.*, **85**, 500 (1963).
45. F. FEIGL and E. BÄCKER, *Monatsh. Chem.*, **49**, 405 (1928).
46. W. C. FERNELIUS and J. E. BLANCH, *Inorganic Syntheses*, Vol. V, McGraw-Hill, New York, 1957, p. 130.
47. A. E. FINN, G. C. HAMPSON and L. E. SUTTON, *J. Chem. Soc.*, 1255 (1938).
48. H. FISCHER and E. BARTHOLAMÄUS, *Ber.*, **45**, 1979 (1912).
49. W. FORSLING, *Acta Chem. Scand.*, **3**, 1133 (1949).
50. H. FRANZEN and W. RYSER, *J. Prakt. Chem.*, **88**, 293 (1913).
51. S. FREED, S. I. WEISSMAN and F. E. FORTESS, *J. Am. Chem. Soc.*, **63**, 1081 (1941).
52. H. FUNK, *Ber.*, **67**, 1801 (1934).
53. C. S. GIBSON and J. L. SIMONSEN, *J. Chem. Soc.*, 2531 (1930).
54. G. GRINER, *Ann. Chim.*, (6) **26**, 305–394 (1892).
55. F. GACH, *Monatsh. Chem.*, **21**, 98, 111, 116 (1900).
56. L. HAHOVEC and K. W. F. KOHLRAUSCH, *Ber.* **73**, 1308 (1940).
56a. G. S. HAMMOND, W. G. BORDUIN and G. A. GUTER, *J. Am. Chem. Soc.*, **81**, 4683 (1959).
56b. G. S. HAMMOND, D. C. NONHEBEL and CHIN-HUA S. WU, *Inorg. Chem.*, **2**, 73 (1963).
57. A. HANTZSCH and C. H. DESCH, *Ann.*, **323**, 18 (1902).
58. B. G. HARVEY, H. G. HEAL, A. G. MADDOCK and E. L. ROWLEY, *J. Chem. Soc.*, 1010 (1947).
59. R. N. HASZELDINE, W. K. R. MUSGRAVE, F. SMITH and L. M. TURTON, *J. Chem. Soc.*, 609 (1951).

60. L. F. Hatch and G. Sutherland, *J. Org. Chem.*, **13**, 252 (1948).
61. A. L. Henne, M. S. Newman, L. L. Quill and R. A. Staniforth, *J. Am. Chem. Soc.*, **69**, 1819 (1947).
62. G. von Hevesy and M. Lögstrup, *Ber.*, **59**, 1890 (1926).
63. W. Hieber, *Sber. Heidelb. Akad.*, No. 3, p. 6 (1929); *C.Z.* 1929I 2030.
64. R. D. Hill, Thesis, University of Manitoba (1962).
64a. H. F. Holtzclaw, Jr. and J. P. Collman, *J. Am. Chem. Soc.* **9**, 3318 (1957).
64b. H. F. Holtzclaw, Jr., K. W. R. Johnson and F. W. Hengeveld, *J. Am. Chem. Soc.*, **74**, 3776 (1952).
64c. H. F. Holtzclaw, Jr., A. H. Carlson and J. P. Collman, *J. Am. Chem. Soc.*, **78**, 1838 (1956).
65. J. P. Howe and W. S. Herbert, *J. Chem. Phys.*, **7**, 219 (1904).
66. N. A. Iljin, *Arch. int. Pharmacol.*, **58**, 378 (1938).
67. F. M. Jaeger, *Proc. Acad. Sci. Amsterdam*, **33**, 280 (1930).
68. F. M. Jaeger, *Rec. Trav. Chim.*, **33**, 388, 394 (1914).
69. G. Jantsch, *J. Prakt. Chem.*, **115**, 7 (1927).
70. G. Jantsch and E. Meyer, *Ber.*, **53**, 1577, 1584 (1920); *Ann.* **323**, 26 (1902).
71. C. James, *J. Am. Chem. Soc.*, **33**, 1332 (1911).
72. A. Job and P. Goissedet, *Compt. rend.*, **157**, 51 (1913).
73. K. I. Karassew, *Z. obsc. Chim.*, **7**, 181 (1937).
74. V. Kohler, *J. Am. Chem. Soc.*, **24**, 355 (1902).
75. E. Kurowski, *Ber.* **43**, 1078 (1910); *J. Russian Phys. Chem.*, **42**, 636 (1910).
76. W. Küster, *Chemie der Zelle und Gewerbe*, **12**, 1–21 (1924).
77. V. Lang, *Z. Kryst. and Mineral.*, **40**, 622 (1904).
77a. E. M. Larson, G. Terry and J. Leddy, *J. Am. Chem. Soc.*, **75**, 5107 (1953).
78. J. Lecomte and R. Freymann, *Compt. rend.*, **208**, 1403 (1939).
79. J. Leroide, *Ann. Chim.*, (9) **16**, 354–410 (1921).
80. H. Ley, *Ber.*, **47**, 2948 (1914).
81. A. G. Maddock and G. L. Miles, *J. Chem. Soc.*, S250 (1949).
82. G. B. Marini-Bettolo and L. Paoloni, *Gazz. Chim. Ital.*, **75**, 85 (1945).
83. J. K. Marsh, *J. Chem. Soc.*, 1084 (1947).
83a. R. K. Mehrotra and R. C. Mehrotra, *Can. J. Chem.*, **39**, 795 (1961).
84. R. C. Menzies, *J. Chem. Soc.*, 2239 (1931); 2606, 2734 (1932); 21 (1933).
85. R. C. Menzies, *J. Chem. Soc.*, 1757 (1934).
86. R. C. Menzies, *J. Chem. Soc.*, 1383 (1947).
87. R. C. Menzies and E. R. Wiltshire, *J. Chem. Soc.*, 2239 (1931); 2606 (1932); 1681 (1936).
88. R. J. Meyer and H. Winter, *Z. anorg. Chem.*, **67**, 398, 414 (1910).
89. A. Michael and G. H. Carlson, *J. Am. Chem. Soc.*, **58**, 356 (1936).
90. J. E. Mills and D. P. Mellor, *J. Am. Chem. Soc.*, **64**, 181 (1942).
91. G. T. Morgan and A. R. Bowen, *J. Chem. Soc.*, **125**, 1259 (1924).
92. G. T. Morgan and R. A. S. Castell, *J. Chem. Soc.*, 3252 (1928).
93. G. T. Morgan and H. D. K. Drew, *J. Chem. Soc.*, **117**, 1460 (1920); **119**, 1058 (1921).
94. G. T. Morgan and H. D. K. Drew, *J. Chem. Soc.*, **121**, 937 (1922).

95. G. T. MORGAN and H. D. K. DREW, *J. Chem. Soc.*, **125**, 784 (1924).
96. G. T. MORGAN and H. D. K. DREW, *J. Chem. Soc.*, **125**, 1261 (1924).
97. G. T. MORGAN, H. D. K. DREW and T. V. BARKER, *J. Chem. Soc.*, **121**, 2432, 2461 (1922).
98. G. T. MORGAN, H. D. K. DREW and C. R. PORTER, *Ber.*, **58**, 333 (1925).
99. G. T. MORGAN and E. HOLMES, *J. Chem Soc.*, **125**, 761 (1924); **127**, 2624, 2894 (1926).
100. G. T. MORGAN and W. LEDBURY, *J. Chem. Soc.*, **121**, 2893 (1922).
101. G. T. MORGAN and H. W. MOSS, *J. Chem. Soc.*, **103**, 88 (1912).
102. G. T. MORGAN and H. W. MOSS, *J. Chem. Soc.*, **105**, 189 (1914).
103. G. T. MORGAN and A. E. RAWSON, *J. Soc. Chem. Ind.*, **44**, 462T (1925).
104. G. T. MORGAN and H. G. REEVES, *J. Chem. Soc.*, **123**, 448 (1922).
105. G. T. MORGAN and R. W. THOMASON, *J. Chem. Soc.*, **125**, 756 (1924).
106. G. T. MORGAN and R. B. TUNSTALL, *J. Chem. Soc.*, **125**, 1963 (1924).
107. M. L. MORRIS, R. W. MOSHIER and R. E. SIEVERS, *Inorg. Chem.*, **2**, 411 (1963).
108. R. A. MORTON and W. C. V. ROSNEY, *J. Chem. Soc.*, 713 (1926).
109. L. PANIZZI, *Gazz. Chim. Ital.*, **71**, 221 (1941).
110. C. L. PARSONS, *J. Am. Chem. Soc.*, **26**, 721–40 (1904).
111. C. L. PARSONS, *Z. anorg. Chem.*, **40**, 412 (1904).
112. J. T. RANDALL, *Nature*, **142**, 113 (1938).
113. J. C. REID and M. CALVIN, *J. Am. Chem. Soc.*, **72**, 2948 (1950).
114. H. REIHLEN, A. GRUHL and G. V. HESSLING, *Ann.*, **472**, 268 (1929).
115. H. REIHLEN, R. ILLIG and R. WITTIG, *Ber.*, **58**, 12 (1925).
116. H. RHEINBOLDT and W. WISFELD, *J. Prakt. Chem.*, **142**, 24 (1935).
117. R. F. RILEY, R. WEST and R. BARBARIN, *Inorganic Syntheses*, Vol. VII, McGraw-Hill, New York, 1963, pp. 30–1.
118. R. A. ROBINSON and D. A. PEAK, *J. Phys. Chem.*, **39**, 1125 (1935).
119. A. ROSENHEIM and A. BERTHEIM, *Z. anorg. Chem.*, **34**, 439.
120. A. ROSENHEIM and A. GARFUNKEL, *Ber.*, **44**, 1870 (1911).
121. A. ROSENHEIM and E. HILZHEIMER and J. WOLFE, *Z. anorg. Chem.*, **201**, 168 (1931).
122. A. ROSENHEIM, W. LÖWENSTAMM and L. SINGER, *Ber.*, **36**, 1836 (1903).
123. A. ROSENHEIM and H. Y. MONG, *Z. anorg. Chem.*, **148**, 25 (1925).
124. A. ROSENHEIM and C. NERNST, *Z. anorg. Chem.*, **214**, 216 (1933).
125. A. ROSENHEIM and E. ROEHRICK, *Z. anorg. Chem.*, **201**, 346 (1931); **204**, 342 (1932).
126. R. A. ROWE, M. M. JONES, B. E. BRYANT and W. C. FERNELIUS, *Inorganic Syntheses*, Vol. V, McGraw-Hill, New York, 1957, pp. 113–5.
127. P. B. SARKAR, *Ann. Chim.*, (10) **8**, 207, 255 (1927); *Bull. Soc. Chim.*, (4), **41**, 187 (1927); **39**, 1391 (1926).
128. A. N. SARKAR, *Phil. Mag.*, (7) **2**, 1153 (1926).
129. G. SCHWARZENBACH and E. FELDER, *Helv. Chim. Acta*, **27**, 1053, 1702 (1944).
130. M. SERVIGNE, *Compt. rend.*, **196**, 264 (1933); *J. Chim. Phys.*, **31**, 47, 55 (1934).
131. R. A. STANIFORTH, Dissertation, Ohio State University, 1943.
132. J. G. STITES, C. H. McCARTY and L. L. QUILL, *J. Am. Chem. Soc.*, **70**, 1085 (1947); **71**, 3142 (1948).

133. S. SUGDEN, *J. Chem. Soc.*, 327 (1929).
134. S. SUGDEN, *J. Chem. Soc.*, 316–30 (1929).
135. S. TANATAR and E. KUROVSKII, *J. Russian Phys. Chem. Soc.*, **40**, 580–4 (1908) *C.Z.* 1908II 1096.
136. S. TANATAR, *J. Russian Phys. Chem. Soc.*, **103**, 86 (1913).
137. G. URBAIN, *Bull. Soc. Chim.*, (3) **15**, 338, 347 (1896).
138. G. URBAIN, *Compt. rend.*, **124**, 618 (1887).
139. G. URBAIN, *Bull. Soc. Chim.*, (3) **15**, 348 (1896).
140. G. URBAIN and A. DEBIERNE, *Compt. rend.*, **129**, 302 (1899).
141. K. C. PANDE and R. C. MEHROLA, *Chem. Ind.*, **35**, 1198 (1958).
142. R. C. MENZIES and A. R. P. WALKER, *J. Chem. Soc.*, 1683 (1936).
143. F. C. WHITMORE and C. E. LEWIS, *J. Am. Chem. Soc.*, **64**, 1619 (1942).
144. A. WERNER, *Ber.* **34**, 2584 (1901).
145. R. WEST, *J. Am. Chem. Soc.*, **80**, 3246 (1958).
146. R. C. YOUNG, *Inorganic Syntheses*, Vol. II, McGraw-Hill, New York, 1946, 25.
147. R. C. YOUNG and A. ARCH, *Inorganic Syntheses*, Vol. II, McGraw-Hill, New York, 1946, 121.
148. R. C. YOUNG, C. GOODMAN and J. KOVITZ, *J. Am. Chem. Soc.*, **61**, 878 (1939).
149. R. C. YOUNG and J. KOVITZ, *Inorganic Syntheses*, Vol. II, McGraw-Hill, New York, 1946, 123.
150. R. C. YOUNG and A. J. V. WEYDEN, *Inorganic Syntheses*, Vol. II, McGraw-Hill, New York, 1946, 119.
151. R. C. YOUNG and A. J. V. WEYDEN, *Inorganic Syntheses*, Vol. II, McGraw-Hill, New York, 1946, 120.
152. G. R. ZELLARS and R. LEVINE, *J. Org. Chem.*, **13**, 161 (1948).
153. Authors' Laboratory, Unpublished data.
154. H. MONTGOMERY and C. E. LINGAFELTER, *Acta Cryst.*, **16**, 748 (1963).
155. D. M. PURI and R. C. MEHROTA, *J. Less-Common Metals*, **3**, 247 (1961); **5**, 2 (1963).

Author Index

155

Subject Index

161

OTHER TITLES IN THE SERIES IN
ANALYTICAL CHEMISTRY